MIKE O'NEAL

REFOCUSED
OUR SAVIOR'S VIEW

21ST CENTURY CHRISTIAN

Refocused
ISBN: 978-0-89098-950-0

©2025 by 21st Century Christian, Inc
Nashville, TN 37215
All rights reserved.

All rights reserved. No part of this publication may be reproduced, stored in a retrieval system, or transmitted in any form or by any means—electronic, mechanical, photocopy, recording, digital, or otherwise—without the written permission of the publisher.

Scripture quotations marked (ESV) are from The Holy Bible, English Standard Version® (ESV®), copyright © 2001 by Crossway, a publishing ministry of Good News Publishers. Used by permission. All rights reserved.

Scripture quotations marked (NASB) are taken from the New American Standard Bible® (NASB), Copyright © 1960, 1962, 1963, 1968, 1971, 1972, 1973, 1975, 1977, 1995 by The Lockman Foundation. Used by permission. lockman.org

Scripture quotations marked (NKJV®) are taken from the New King James Version®. Copyright © 1982 by Thomas Nelson, Inc. Used by permission. All rights reserved.

Cover design by Jared Kendall

Table of Contents

Preface and Acknowledgements 5

CHAPTER ONE
Seeing & 'Touching' Insights 11

CHAPTER TWO
A 'Short' Story 31

CHAPTER THREE
Blind-Sighted 47

CHAPTER FOUR
Sympathetic Eyes 69

CHAPTER FIVE
A Shepherd's View 91

CHAPTER SIX
Some Perspectives on Widows 109

CHAPTER SEVEN
A Look of Concern 129

Endnotes 143

ENDORSEMENTS

Like prescription eyeglasses or cataract surgery, they give you 20/20 vision. *Refocused* improves the eyes of your heart with every page. It was the new exam and prescription I needed. In this book, writer Mike O'Neal pulls back the curtains of cloudiness to help you see like Jesus. Every chapter provides a clearer look at life. Thank you, Mike, for performing the surgery I needed to see from the perspective of Jesus. Optics, it's all about perspective!
—**James Moore,** Retired, President,
Mount Dora Christian Academy and Children's Home

All of Michael O'Neal's previous books are well-researched and offer unique perspectives on significant spiritual themes. This one is no different. Here he challenges us to view friends, neighbors, and all others through the eyes (perspective) of Jesus as He is presented in the Gospels.
—**Dr. Allen Black,** Professor of New Testament Emeritus,
Harding School of Theology

Refocused brings together several significant stories from Jesus' ministry and invites us to train our eyes to see what Jesus saw. How did He perceive and receive the people around Him? Full of heartfelt stories and thoughtful considerations, Mike's work here will bless you and help you to be more like Jesus.
—**Dr. Mark Adams,** Preaching Minister, Tusculum Church of Christ,
Nashville, TN

PREFACE AND ACKNOWLEDGEMENTS

As an author, you sometimes come across a passage, phrase, or a word that seems to jump up and down and shout, "Look at me! Look at me!" This book's genesis came through such vociferous words. Over a short period of time, I took note of many verses where Jesus "saw," "observed," or "looked" upon someone and their surrounding circumstances. He would subsequently act and/or say things that might be quite different from His apostles or the other characters in the story. It dawned on me how important it is to understand Jesus' perspectives and how we need to align our spiritual eyesight with His. We often see others so differently than Jesus would, even if we notice them at all. These stories help bring to light our poor eyesight and challenge us to refocus our vision and align it with Jesus'. If becoming like Jesus is our goal, our path to this noble aim will be obstructed if we do not embrace His perspectives.

I seldom undertake writing something that I am not passionate about. Passion drives my joy, and when it is not present, joy is sucked right out of my life. For me, writing is a good deed that I perform for you. Good works need to be powered by zeal (Titus 2:14), and if it is not present, we should question whether to undertake it. The spiritual formation twists related to this topic, and within these stories, started to spark my zeal. Not much time passed, and I told my wife that I needed to write a book on this topic. My creative energies were put to the test, as it took several years to assemble this book in a meaningful way. I hope you'll find some fresh takes on some old stories and will be intrigued and challenged by this material.

Like my previous four books, you will find that I enjoy using contemporary stories to illustrate the technical concepts of the biblical text. The majority of these stories come from my own personal experiences in a diverse array of life, such as working in the space program, raising children, hiking, dealing with friends, encountering various situations at church, and watching or participating in sports. These stories allow me to introduce new material and demonstrate the biblical concepts and principles with present-day examples. I also include a section at the end of each chapter titled, "Illuminating Thoughts," that solely deals with the application of the themes presented in the chapter. A few times, I used interviews from subject-matter experts within this section to draw your attention to some lessons learned from these authoritative individuals. The running text also contains material from interviews to further enlighten the reader and provide added depth to the themes in the book.

I am grateful to all who agreed to be interviewed. Your expertise, life experiences, and practical insights provided a dimension to the book that I could not have achieved without you. I believe the readers will be blessed by the sharing of your stories and insights. A few of those interviewed, I mentioned by name in the book, but others, I have chosen to keep anonymous for various reasons.

Preface and Acknowledgements

One thing you can count on for sure, before I sit down at a keyboard and start typing, I've conducted a tremendous amount of research. I am accountable to God for what I write and teach to you. Once I have a rudimentary concept of the book, I spend many hours researching the various topics in the library at the Harding School of Theology (HST) in Memphis, Tennessee. I bring back a tremendous amount of material to read multiple times, as I develop each chapter. From this material, and my own personal library, if I am unsure about a particular biblical teaching or the nuance of a Greek/Hebrew word or phrase, I contact an appropriate expert to help me derive the proper understanding.

Because I'm an alumnus of HST, the librarians worked tirelessly to help me obtain some of the material that I needed. I find them to be some of the finest unsung heroes in the world of Christian literature. I would like to specifically thank the former dean, Allen Black, of this august institution for helping me properly interpret some difficult Greek words and phrases.

The wonderful story about John Glenn that sets the book in motion was shared with me by my good friend and NASA colleague, Jack Fox. He not only provided this eye-opening story but offered other thoughtful ideas as well. I truly appreciate your encouragement during this journey.

My good friend, Gayle Griffin, spent many hours scouring this book for editorial problems. My raw writing style comes with a few rough edges, and her skillful and thoughtful review has helped make this work a more appealing read. Sometimes we do not think of some of the things we do in life as a ministry, but her devoted service in this capacity has served both you and me, as well as our amazing God. Her assistance has helped me put together a study that will hopefully be useful to you in your spiritual development. Gayle, I know the time and energy that you expended on this book has taken you away from your loved ones and personal interests.

In all earnestness, I thank you for your sacrifices and contribution to *Refocused*.

I am also grateful to my minister friends, Mike Shumate, Jerry Starling, Mark Adams, and Bob Bliss. Each of them provided guidance and validation on many of the approaches that I took in the book, as well as some specific insights concerning the biblical text. Mike also served as a subject-matter expert in some of the human behavioral matters that I address throughout the book. His service as a PhD Christian Counselor was extremely helpful in making sure that I properly handled those items. Thank all of you for providing a listening ear and thoughtful remarks.

My wife walked by my side throughout this journey, especially allowing me to read aloud sections of the manuscript to her, as well as discussing some of the concepts for the book. Your patient listening had a positive impact on the book, and I know this often occurred, when you were tired or took you away from other activities. I am forever thankful for your support and reading each completed chapter.

It may seem out of place, but I want to thank my publisher, 21st Century Christian. Thank you so much for allowing me to serve God in a writing capacity. Your company has personally blessed me in many ways, and I am truly grateful that you put your faith in me to put this project together. Through the years, I have truly felt love and encouragement from many of your workers. Stacey Owens, my technical editor, is a pro's pro and is to be commended for her skills and thoughtful advice. Stacey, your work is a true service to God's kingdom, and an Acknowledgements section would be incomplete without saying so.

Lastly, to the readers, I thank you for studying this book. As a writer, I find it humbling for others to spend their valuable time exploring the pages of my books. I can assure you that this book was a work of passion, was prayed over, and is well-researched. I truly believe that you will be spiritually enriched by its contents. I pray that God will draw you closer to Him and help align your spiritual vision with His Son's, as you delve into the pages of this book.

To my loving God and Jesus, I praise Your holy names and offer thanksgiving and all the glory to You. Thank You for Your wonderful Word. It's truly illuminating!

CHAPTER ONE

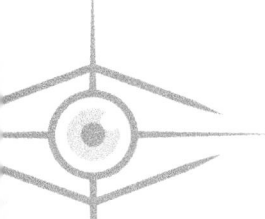

SEEING & 'TOUCHING' INSIGHTS

The precepts of the LORD are right, rejoicing the heart;
The commandment of the LORD is pure, enlightening the eyes
—Psalm 19:8.

Prior to John Glenn's Space Shuttle flight, a good friend and colleague of mine had the privilege of touring the honorable senator around the Kennedy Space Center (KSC). Many years had passed since Glenn's Mercury mission, so a detailed tour of KSC's facilities was in order. One of the stops included the Engineering Development Laboratory, where my friend had a flight experiment undergoing tests. It was destined to be flown on Glenn's mission, where it would be demonstrated for potential incorporation into the Shuttle fleet. After learning about this promising technology, they exited the lab and started to make their way to the next tour stop. While briskly progressing down a long corridor, Glenn noticed an elderly janitor meekly approaching his group while pushing a trash container. The older gentleman started to hug the wall, as he drew near to the sea of suits that encompassed Glenn. Without warning, this legendary test pilot speedily broke through the ranks of his entourage of about 15 people, like he was bursting through the sound barrier again, and made a beeline toward the custodian. As a former astronaut who piloted his Mercury capsule to become the first American to orbit the Earth, he now navigated his way to a rendezvous with this unsuspecting man. Glenn met him head-on and immediately clasped the hand of the shocked janitor and eagerly shook it. After cursory introductions, the inquisitive senator asked him to share a few things about himself. Glenn's eyes became riveted on his newfound friend, and he paid close attention to every word, as the custodian disclosed some things about his tenure at the space center. When the man stated that he had worked in the space program for about 30 years, Glenn launched into an impassioned message of gratitude. This American hero emphatically told the custodian that "he should be proud of himself!" That he was a part of and contributed to a much greater team — a team that accomplished many remarkable things through the years. Still clasping the custodian's hand, Glenn continued to look into his eyes, as he thanked him for his service and then bid him farewell and rejoined his group of dignitaries.

My friend's jaw dropped as he witnessed this entire conversation. He said sincerity, appreciation, and humility oozed out of Glenn's pores. Votes were not the motivation for this senator from Ohio, his care for this Floridian was genuine and a natural extension of who he was. He *saw* value in this man's contributions and in the man himself. My colleague had seen many remarkable things while at NASA, but perhaps none more impressed him than Glenn's wonderful treatment of this janitor.

Glenn's story begs a few questions for us to entertain. Would we have noticed this janitor? If so, how would we have viewed him? Would a callous judgmentalism have shaped our view of his occupation as distasteful and precipitated our assessment of his personhood as well? Without even knowing this man might we have quickly categorized and marginalized him as a person? What causes us to *see* others the way that we do? In the coming pages, we will explore this phenomenon. We will specifically investigate several biblical stories to determine how Jesus *saw* others. Obviously, seeing people through a lens of concern and compassion is always a seminal trait in shaping Jesus' perspectives. When possible, we will compare Jesus' "seeing" with the flawed views of other characters in the stories. Ultimately, we need to refocus our eyes to address our own faulty vision. This will hopefully facilitate the Spirit's transformative work in each of us, as we pursue seeing others and the world around us like our Savior.

SIGHT DEFICIENCIES

When it comes to "seeing," Paul provided some helpful insights to the church at Corinth that can still serve us today. To help establish and create unity, he told them that God gave various spiritual gifts to their brothers and sisters at their church. Unfortunately, rather than creating unity, a culture of division and one-upmanship developed. One of the gifts he mentioned was that of "the word of knowledge" (1 Corinthians 12:8). Paul went on to explain in 1 Corinthians 13 the importance of practicing their gifts in loving ways. Concerning those who had the gift involving knowledge, he basically said, "Even if you are all-knowing but treat people in unloving ways, you are nothing" (see 1 Corinthians 13:2). Some with this gift probably had a "know-it-all" attitude and treated others without it as inferior and perhaps even with disdain. In verse 9, he clarified that they only "know in part," or in other words, "their knowledge fell far short of all-knowing." This brings us to a statement that bears closer examination.

> For now we see in a mirror dimly, but then face to face; now I know in part, but then I shall know fully, even as I have been fully known (v. 12).

Corinth was well-known in the ancient world for fashioning high-quality bronze mirrors. As such, Paul would have been careful to avoid insulting their craftsmanship, so he was not suggesting that a mirror produced hazy or distorted images. Rather, his thought was that reflections give incomplete or indirect images. His point was that their knowledge was like a reflection; it was incomplete and not like seeing something "face to face" in all its detail. The "now" and "then" language of the verse is likely dealing with the difference between their current state and their existence at their consummation.[1]

Photographs provide a similar analogy to that of a mirror. Pictures tell an incomplete story. For example, I have never seen a picture that truly reflects the beauty of Yellowstone's Grand Canyon. The natural splendor, the vibrancy of the many colors, the panoramic magnificence, and the vast span of the dimensions are just not adequately captured in a photograph. Only by observing and experiencing this scene in person can one truly comprehend the canyon's breathtaking beauty. Of course, any photograph presents similar issues. They fall short of the eyewitness experience. A photograph's two-dimensional features provide us with a lot of information but possess limitations.

SIGHT-SHAPING FEATURES

Even though Paul's context was different, his principle still serves to remind us today that our "seeing" also falls short in several ways. We will not attempt to examine an exhaustive list of the features that affect our vision but will instead look at a representative set of these sight-shaping items for you to better understand their role in how you perceive others and the world. Also, it isn't my intent to explore their genesis but for you to understand their presence and influence.

Some of these features took many years to take shape and were engendered by our parents, friends, family, teachers, culture, life experiences, peers, and the like. As our eyes take in the physical aspects of our environment, our brain utilizes these sight-shaping features to rapidly categorize, frame, type, and determine relevancy and priority of what we are encountering.[2] From the perceptions produced, behaviors will then ensue, allowing us to navigate the circumstances and individuals that surround us. For instance, if we come around the corner of a building and behold a homeless man, we may immediately give him a wide berth. We do this because we view him as unsafe or do not want to be bothered by his panhandling. Also, these features will continue to be at work, as we form our opinions and learn to deal with the people in our lives and the situations that we face.

Paul's comment to the Corinthians serves to directly point us to our first sight-shaping feature to consider. We are not all-knowing and often work on *incomplete information*. This feature manifests itself in many ways, but perhaps none is more insidious than our "superhuman" ability to judge the intentions of the hearts of others (healthy dose of sarcasm here). For example, we come home from work, dreading the task of washing a pile of dirty dishes that we left in the sink from the night before, only to find them sparkling clean and drying in the dish rack. We could jump to the conclusion that our daughter lovingly thought of us and did not want us to come home to such a mess. The truth reveals an underlying bitterness in her attitude: The daughter washed them in disgust. She had a friend coming over, and the odor of seafood on the dirty dishes was revolting and embarrassing to her. Undoubtedly, we become familiar with some folks in our lives and have an inkling of their possible intentions. I have often correctly deduced the motives of someone I know reasonably well, but many times, I have mistakenly misread them and jumped to the wrong conclusions . . . sometimes shamefully.

Our perceptions are constantly misled by our lack of information. Perhaps you can relate to some of the following examples. We think a friend is avoiding us for something we did, when that avoidance simply stems from a desire to keep to themselves because they just don't feel well. We see a new acquaintance approaching in a New York Yankees hat, and we assume that he is an avid fan of this team. The truth is that he abhors them and begrudgingly borrowed the hat to protect his face from the sun. Based on a suspicious incident, we jump to the conclusion that one of our buddies acted unethically per a trusted friend's report. Later, we learn some additional information from another reliable confidant making us realize that everything really was above-board.

We all have made errors in judgment based on inadequate information. Consequently, this has caused us to backtrack and revise our opinions, change our decisions, and even ask for forgiveness for unjust behaviors. Let's always be careful in jumping to conclusions about others and acting rashly, knowing that insufficient information distorts and perverts our perceptions.

A second feature that distorts our sight is *incorrect information*. Misinformation can slip into our thought-world in several ways. Most obviously, others can lie to us. Their motivations may vary. Have you ever experienced any of the following? A friend decided to deceive you, because they were ashamed of something they did and did not want you to think poorly of them. A relative was undergoing a divorce and misled you as to the circumstances in the hopes of justifying their actions in your eyes. A mean-spirited individual, who did not like you, insultingly exaggerated something about your appearance to harm your self-image. An acquaintance desiring money for drugs lied to you about the real reason they wanted it. Some people are remarkably good liars, and their clever fabrications have fooled me on several occasions.

Sometimes we are innocently, or recklessly, given incorrect information. For example, have you had a friend truly believe what they are telling you is the truth, but you knew, or later learned, their words were false? They may have unknowingly misinterpreted the circumstances surrounding an event and passed it on to you as fact. Biases and prejudices can cause them to see others and situations through a lens that can easily cause them to misconstrue information. Because of misguided care for you, a friend may misrepresent a bad attribute of yours to avoid any confrontation. Rather than dealing with the character issue head-on, they try to get you to believe that you are something you aren't. One of my pet peeves is the adage that "we can do anything that we put our mind to" in life. Perhaps well-intentioned, this is just not always the case. I would love to play professional basketball, but I am too short and not fast enough. No amount of practice and training will allow me to play in the NBA. I may be a rocket scientist, but I just do not have the fine motor skills and intellectual capacity to be a brain surgeon. Practically speaking, we all have limitations. Yes, we should have goals that stretch and challenge us, but they must also be reasonable. If not, individuals can act on such misinformation, only to later be disheartened and disappointed.

Sadly, a few years ago, I heard a new phrase: "fake news." It's horrible to think that others in our world are strategically concocting lies, creating phony stories, and deceptively presenting information to shape our thinking. They want us to believe and act in certain ways, and their own personal ethics do not prevent them from feeding you misinformation. Personally, lack of integrity in our society is repugnant. Knowing your sources and checking up on the facts is a wise approach, so we can make sound judgments and act judiciously. Whether malicious or innocent, incorrect information can easily distort our vision.

A third sight-shaping feature that influences our vision concerns our deeply held *beliefs and values*. These core beliefs help us make meaning of the things we encounter in life and determine what is important to us. Not only does this feature consist of our values, but also includes *what* we value. What we place our faith and trust in serves to fashion our attitudes and passions in significant ways. A case in point, integrity is a core value of mine. If someone tries to force me to oppose this ethic, I will likely challenge them on their tactics and avoid partnering with them on specific activities in the future.

We are typically attracted to individuals of like faith. While on vacation once, I saw a man putting something into his car in a parking lot, and my eyes were suddenly attracted to a sticker on his back window. Its message was succinct and powerful; "He >me" (He is greater than me). I enthusiastically shouted over to him, "Hey, I like that sticker!" He looked up and flashed a smile at me and replied, "Yeah, it's true all the time." I then offered a hearty, "Amen!" On first take, I could see myself befriending this man, whom I had never met, because of a common belief that we shared.

Fellow members of any congregation will be bonded together by deeply held common beliefs. Nevertheless, there will always be differences regarding what is important to them. Experience has taught me that some of those differences can cause us to seek like-minded individuals in whom we can place our trust — often in healthy ways but sometimes in unhealthy ways. I am sure most of us can relate to this. These shared beliefs allow them to find mutual support in one another and permit them to safely talk about their passions, interests, and issues related to these matters-of-faith.

A fourth feature that affects our seeing involves our *likes and dislikes, prejudices, and biases.* Important people in our lives and significant life experiences have helped form these aspects of our identity. By the way, our "likes" are not necessarily good, and most "likes" necessitate a "dislike." Many years ago, a fellow member of a church I was attending made a distasteful comment that I will never forget. After I expressed some concerns about our congregation's lack of growth, he responded with something like, "Growth. I do not want any growth. Our church is the ideal size." Not sure I know what the "ideal size" of a church is, but I am certain that we have a biblical mandate to grow them. His "like" of an "ideal-sized" church came with the "dislike" of anything that differed. Likes and dislikes influence our behaviors. I don't know how this person's likes and dislikes specifically affected him, but I cannot see how it could be positive. He probably did not try to run off visitors, but he may have exhibited an attitude of indifference toward them.

My dad raised me as a Baltimore Orioles baseball fan. He did an extraordinary job, as I am a die-hard one. This "like" has stuck with me for a lifetime. As I have worn my Oriole gear around the country, every so often I will be greeted with a "Go O's!" from somewhere nearby. Looking around to give my hearty approval to the person who showed admiration to my beloved team often turns into a passion-filled conversation. The fellowship of "likes" not only comes with some strong natural attractions, but often opens the door to new heartfelt friendships.

Sometimes others try to figure out points of likeness with us, so they can relate to us on some level. New at a particular church, my wife and I stood next to a long-standing member in a long line for a potluck meal. Recognizing us as a recent addition, she struck up a conversation with me, and it wasn't long before she asked, "Do you like bluegrass music?" I hesitantly responded, "Not really, I prefer rock-and-roll." My response impeded our conversation at the time, but on the long-haul, our common faith allowed our relationship to flourish. My newfound friend played the mandolin in a bluegrass band called the Skeeter Beaters, and she could not help but introduce me to this amusing genre of music. Still to my surprise, I, a die-hard rock-and-roller, came to enjoy a little bluegrass now and then.

Sometimes our desire for inclusion with a particular group of people may cause prejudices to arise. Some people outside the group may be viewed as adversaries, or their differences are seen as inferior or undesirable. Such prejudices are often fraught with incomplete and incorrect information. Alliances within groups are powerful and can have deep tendrils into our identity.

Typically, our likes and dislikes may be harmless; it's the behaviors they produce that may be un-Christian. But having prejudices against people is un-Christian. God probably has a lot of transformative work to perform with most of us in this regard.

Our last sight-shaping feature involves *safety and fear*. Concerning people, we will be attracted to those we deem safe. For example, if we come upon a couple of co-workers incessantly gossiping about someone, you will likely never trust them with confidential information about yourself. Such info may just be juicy fodder for them to share with a friend. We will hopefully be attracted to trustworthy confidants.

Our initial impression of someone's appearance will often determine if we feel that we need to avoid them. If a woman is making her way to her car in a mall parking lot, and a man with skulls on his shirt and tattoos on his arms is approaching her, she may deem him as unsafe. She may speedily get into her car, or do an about face, and head back into the mall. Fear is a powerful motivator in how we choose to behave.

Again, the goal of this section is to familiarize us with how our brain uses these features to shape our perceptions. This list is not meant to be exhaustive. You probably already noted how some of these features may overlap and work in harmony or conflict with one another. Please be aware of their presence, as some of these sight-shapers will need re-shaping. God has given His people the ultimate Re-shaper to help us address our sight issues — His Spirit. We just need to be aware of them and possess the desire to change those that are inconsistent with our Christianity and be on guard against any bad behaviors that they may produce.

Let's look at a short story, where we can see how Jesus responded to an individual in a way that assuredly astounded those around Him. That will be our goal in the coming chapters: to uncover how Jesus perceives others and subsequently treats them. We need to spiritually search deep within ourselves to understand if our "seeing" would be consistent with His.

TOUCHING INSIGHTS

Growing up in Florida was wonderful, primarily because I spent a lot of time outside throughout the year. Going to the beach, playing sports, and mowing lawns for money were some of my core activities as a teen. Bleached-out blond hair and dark tans were the norm for me in the summer months. Unfortunately, suntan lotions did not contain good sunscreens back then, so my skin took in a lot of sun. This lifestyle caught up with me in my 40s, as I started to develop an issue with various skin cancers. At one point, my dermatologist prescribed a cream for use on my forehead that was designed to have one's immune system attack and destroy any precancerous skin cells that were present. After only a week of treatment, my skin reacted severely to the ointment, and a scab marched its way across my entire forehead. I looked grotesque and felt embarrassed by my appearance. NASA let me work from home for a couple weeks while my skin recovered. My isolation from others was short-lived, yet almost unbearable for an active person like me. Can you imagine if you experienced such a malady that went on for years? Such was the case for one woman in Scripture.

Compassion had Jesus on the move (Mark 5:21–43). Jairus's daughter was dying, and this desperate synagogue official begged Jesus to make haste and come to his home to heal her. So off Jesus went, but a spectacle ensued. A "great multitude" of onlookers paraded along and pressed in on Jesus as He went; obviously, hoping to be present if Jesus performed a miracle. Jesus' urgent mission of mercy took an unexpected and abrupt turn, as someone from the crowd secretly, and desperately, reached out to the Savior for healing.

> A woman who had had a hemorrhage for twelve years, and had endured much at the hands of many physicians, and had spent all that she had and was not helped at all, but rather had grown worse — after hearing about Jesus, she came up in the crowd behind *Him* and touched His cloak. For she thought, "If I just touch His garments, I will get well." Immediately the flow of her blood was dried up; and she felt in her body that she was healed of her affliction. Immediately Jesus, perceiving in Himself that the power *proceeding* from Him had gone forth, turned around in the crowd and said, "Who touched My garments?" And His disciples said to Him, "You see the crowd pressing in on You, and You say, 'Who touched Me?'" And He looked around to see the woman who had done this. But the woman fearing and trembling, aware of what had happened to her, came and fell down before Him and told Him the whole truth. And He said to her, "Daughter, your faith has made you well; go in peace and be healed of your affliction" (Mark 5:25–34).

Plight of the Woman

We need to ask a few questions about this anonymous woman to better understand her plight and Jesus' reaction. Why was she so stealthy? Why spend "all" her money in search of a cure while suffering at the hands of "many" doctors? Why include the details that she had had the hemorrhage for 12 years and was now worse? Why respond with fear and trembling at her discovery? Mark painted a picture of desperation, but did his readers understand something that we may not?

Undoubtedly, Mark has described a woman who was afflicted with a continuous menstrual hemorrhage that had left her ritually unclean (see Leviticus 15:19–30).[3] Her constant loss of blood likely left her in a weakened state, which was further aggravated by the doctors worsening her condition. Her suffering, though, ran much deeper. For 12 years, her malady left her societally and religiously isolated. Twelve years!! Anything and anyone she touched would have been left unclean. She lived as an outcast and surely endured much disdain and humiliation by her own people. So yes, she was desperate — really desperate — and emotionally in deep pain. She needed a Savior.

Basically, this woman had no hope. The doctors could not heal her. Furthermore, even if a new treatment became available, she had no money left to gain access to it. She lived in isolation with the shame of her uncleanness constantly before her. She depended on others to go to the marketplace and procure food for her. Her ritual uncleanness kept her from worshiping God at the synagogue. Assuredly, she felt physically exhausted all the time as well. Her life was a living nightmare. Then she heard the remarkable news that was abuzz amongst her people; great multitudes, from not only Judea and Galilee, but from surrounding countries, were going to this miracle worker for healing (Mark 3:7–10). Moreover, great fortune was coming her way, as this Jesus was destined to come through her town. Invigorated with a fresh hope, this anguished woman became emboldened to step out on faith. Remember, our hope in what God has done for us through Jesus should truly embolden us to step out on faith as well.

Why the stealthy approach? As a woman, her cultural norms hindered her from pleading her case before Jesus, but this goes beyond such conventions. Her unclean status not only restricted her from such public gatherings, but touching Jesus would leave Him unclean. Probably with veil over her face, and in the anonymity of this large crowd, she approached Him from behind to avoid detection and inconspicuously touched the fringe of His garment

(Luke 8:44). Intense desperation caused her to choose her secretive and scandalous tactics.[4]

Jesus' Response

Amazingly, and perhaps alarmingly, she immediately knew that she was at last healed. While thinking, *Now, just to slip back out of this crowd unnoticed*, she discreetly withdrew her hand from Jesus. What happened next left her mortified. Jesus had felt the healing power flow from Him and turned toward the crowd and asked, "Who touched My garments?" (v. 30). Stunned by her detection, the woman momentarily remained quiet, but then Jesus met her gaze. What Jesus saw in her eyes said it all. Trembling in pure dread of having been discovered, along with a fearful awe of Jesus' powers, she fell at His feet and told Him the "whole truth" of the plight that drove her behavior. She also surely disclosed the dehumanizing nature of her disease and her conviction that she would receive healing through Him.

Since her identity was revealed, the crowd probably started angrily murmuring and backing away from this unclean, destitute woman. The apostles stood with mouths agape, wondering how Jesus knew of her touch and knowing they would have to deal with His unclean state. No one understood that Jesus' healing powers not only healed her but kept Him clean as well.

Her fear may have precipitated concerns for how Jesus would respond. Perhaps, her mind screamed out in a frenzied panic, *Oh no, I violated the purity laws, illegitimately stole His power,[5] and broke the barriers concerning interaction with men - shamefully, public chastisement awaits me.* Even the ultimate of horrors may have intruded on her fear-filled mind, *Will He take away my healing and return me to my former hopeless state?* Little did she realize at the moment that good fortune awaited her, because compassion resided in the core of the One in whom she placed her faith.

Shockingly, Jesus admired the woman. No chastisement, no ridicule, no abuses proceeded from His mouth. Instead, He affectionately referred to her as "daughter" and held up her faith as an example before the crowd and all ages to come. To Jesus, her unwavering faith in Him made her family, as He earlier explained:

> Answering them, He said, "Who are My mother and My brothers?" Looking around at those who were sitting around Him, He said, "Here are My mother and My brothers! For whoever does the will of God, this is My brother, and sister, and mother" (Mark 3:33–35).

Excluded and marginalized for years by her own people, Jesus saw this ostracized woman through the eyes of compassion and now included her as family. Designed to protect them from uncleanness, the law was not intended to dehumanize anyone.[6] Jesus broke down some barriers and showed the woman acceptance and inclusiveness that she had not felt for years. Not only did His actions let everyone know that He cared about the plight of this woman, but He also understood her pain and cared about her as an individual — something she treasured in her heart.

Rather than scolding her, Jesus blessed the woman, giving her peace and a healing that would last. To the Jews, peace conveyed a sense of "wholeness" and "well-being." Jesus' blessing assured this woman that her life had taken a renewed and revitalized turn. Trusting in Jesus has a way of doing that for us all.

ILLUMINATING THOUGHTS

In our story, the disciples' response is not unexpected. Only Jesus knew that His healing power had flown from Himself to someone else, so when He asked, "Who touched my garments" they must have thought, *You've got to be kidding me! Come on Jesus, this crazy crowd cannot stop themselves from reaching out to touch You — How could You ever single out just one of them?* Yet, He did! The disciples saw a crowd. Jesus saw people. The disciples saw chaos. Jesus saw individuals in need of an eye-opening lesson.

We encounter crowds of people throughout our lives. At times, they may physically be before us, and at other times, they are the collective people that vie for our attention. We must ask ourselves, *"Do we see those who are in need or do we see just a crowd or chaos? Like Jesus, are we inclusive and willing to help even an outcast?"* Paul pointed out to the churches in Rome that the differences and pasts of our Christian brothers and sisters should not cause us to deny them our fellowship or to ignore their needs.

> Therefore, accept one another, just as Christ also accepted us, for the glory of God (Romans 15:7).

The Greek word for *accept* conveys warmth, welcoming, and wholehearted acceptance.[7] Christ accepts us in such a manner. Therefore, we need to develop such an attitude, as we accept others as well. Such loving acceptance brings glory to God.

As high school senior, I was the president of a club called Interact. The principal that year decided to institute a new policy concerning selecting new members for the clubs — 50 percent could be directly selected, but the other 50 percent were to be chosen at random. To lose control over who could join our group was quite upsetting to our membership. Nevertheless, I'll never forget the profound impact this process had on two of our random selectees. Socially awkward, these two young men would not have survived our direct selection process. After pulling their names out of a baseball hat, I told them of their addition to our club - both were overjoyed. Our group truly welcomed them, and they responded with spirited enthusiasm. They joined the ranks of a few that "vigorously" participated in all our activities. Their acceptance brought about a remarkable joy in these young men, which led to extremely devoted behaviors. Acceptance and inclusiveness are powerful and sincerely sought after by many people. This lesson has stuck with me for a lifetime.

On Sunday morning when service has ended, take it upon yourself to seek out those standing alone and not talking to anyone. Strike up a conversation with them. Get to know them. Come to care about them. Share a meal with them and let the warmth of acceptance flow. We need to build bonds of trust with others, so they will be upfront about their deep hurts and needs. Perhaps then, they will let us in to minister to them.

"See" those around you . . . refocus on them and let your acceptance flow.

QUESTIONS

1. In the story at the beginning of the chapter, why do you think John Glenn reacted the way he did with the janitor? How do you think the janitor felt afterward?

2. Of the five sight-shaping features mentioned, what one tends to cause you the most problems in properly "seeing" others? How should you address this?

3. Try to recall a time when either the lack of information or misinformation caused you to wrongly deduce something about a friend or colleague. What led to your wrong conclusions? What could you have done differently?

4. How important are your faith and values in driving your behaviors? Where might you have some shortcomings in these areas?

Seeing & 'Touching' Insights

5. How did the Jews of Jesus' day likely "see" the woman with the hemorrhage? Why? How would they have treated her? Describe her life.

6. Were you surprised by Jesus' response to the woman touching Him in the crowd? What did Jesus accomplish with His response? Is there someone today reaching out to you in some way? How might you respond?

CHAPTER TWO

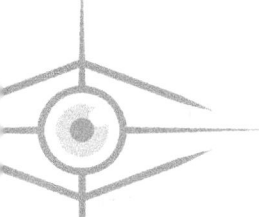

A 'SHORT' STORY

When the Pharisees saw this, they said to His disciples, "Why is your Teacher eating with the tax collectors and sinners?"
—Matthew 9:11.

Many years ago, I yearned for the day that free agency would arrive for a particular baseball star. I just knew that he was destined to sign with my beloved team, the Orioles. He grew up in the Baltimore area, and supposedly, the Os were his favorite childhood team. He stated that he would love to play for them, and that it would be a dream come true. When his free agency finally came about and he could choose from several suitors, it was then up to the Orioles' front office to make an amenable offer. Not too surprisingly, the Os executives made a monumental, long-term offer. In my heart of hearts, I just knew this perennial all-star would soon be donning an Orioles cap and jersey.

A short time later, I learned that he had signed with the New York Yankees. As I remember, the amount of money was close to the same per year, but the Yankees outmaneuvered the Orioles' front office by adding an extra year. In no uncertain terms, the Os offered this man a treasure chest full of money. So how could a devoted Orioles enthusiast sign with a team that was their mortal enemy? To me, he was a traitor. To the fans, he was a traitor. In the coming games in Baltimore, boos rained down in a deafening fashion throughout the entire stadium, whenever this turncoat came up to bat. The Yankees' proposal aside, the amount of money the Orioles offered him would have made him filthy rich. So how could he have made such a disloyal choice? He was a traitor!

Such experiences are not uncommon. Allegiances to our cherished sports teams often run deep and can bring about some unhealthy emotions when they are dishonored. Let's take that same fervent loyalty and magnify it. In your eyes, how would you feel about someone who was disloyal to their (and your) country, while potentially turning their back on their (and your) religion? Your life circumstances are degraded by this individual's unfaithful ways, and you see them on a regular basis, living prosperously at your expense. Jesus encountered such a situation, and we can learn from how He perceived and handled it, knowing greater issues were at stake. But first let's look at how "seeing" and the heart are related.

SEEING AND THE HEART

Paul's prayer for the Christians in Ephesus that God would enlighten "the eyes of your heart" (Ephesians 1:18) conveys some seminal ideas for our study. In this specific instance, he desired that their hearts would be grounded in the benefits of the gospel through what God had done for them in Christ Jesus. However, let's look at this phrase in a broader way. First, note that their spiritual eyes (eyes of the heart) were not fully matured, which points to the need for their continued development.[8] Later, Paul again prayed for the Ephesians, asking God to strengthen them "with power through His Spirit in the inner man, so that Christ may dwell in your hearts through faith . . ." (Ephesians 3:16–17). Again, we see Paul praying for further development of their hearts. Paul specifically stated to the Corinthians that the Spirit is placed in our hearts (2 Corinthians 1:22). That is where the Spirit performs His work, as we are progressed from one glory to the next in our transformation to Christlikeness (2 Corinthians 3:18). We basically are in a partnership with God's Spirit. As we desire to become more like Christ and present to the Spirit some fertile ground with which to work, He fashions our hearts as needed. This progression is a lifelong journey that will not be completed this side of heaven.

Second, our spiritual eyes see through the lens that our hearts provide. Whether corrupt or godly, our heart shapes our sight. So, what is the heart? From a biblical standpoint, the heart is quite complicated, involving the personality, thoughts, desires, emotions, will, beliefs, and moral codes. Spiritually, the heart is our spiritual and moral center, influencing our choices, as it helps us navigate life. So, how does a *selfish* versus a *selfless* heart influence our approach with those around us? Rather than looking out for the interests of others, a selfish heart determines how to use them to achieve its goals and look good. In other words, a selfish heart objectifies others. To the contrary, a selfless heart sees the needs of others and yearns to sacrificially address them before focusing on its own desires. A greedy heart views others as tools to help them become prosperous; whereas, a giving heart sacrificially reaches out to the impoverished to help them meet their dire needs.[9]

Like me, I am sure you realize that some serious flaws remain in our hearts. We must be patient with their development. God chose not to enact change upon our hearts without our desiring it and following a path to facilitate it. That is why it is a progression, not an all-at-once momentary change. We cannot force this change on our own, and God does not force it on His own. Yes, to see others properly, we need "enlightenment," "transformation," and for Christ to "dwell in our hearts." Remember, hope is ever before us, and God's power resides in us. We should keep pressing on and address those issues of the heart that obscure our *vision*. Let's now explore how Jesus *sees* a hated man in great need and how our *sight* may need adjusting.

LOOKING UP

Luke imparted to us one of the most endearing stories in the Bible — the story of Zaccheus's conversion. If you ever attended Vacation Bible School, you likely, and excitedly, sang, "Zaccheus was a wee little man and a wee little man was he . . ." Even with the charm of a "wee" little man climbing a sycamore tree to see Jesus, this story conveys some serious and vital lessons for its readers; especially when it comes to "seeing." In 10 short verses, Luke provided the highlights of a story that likely occurred over many hours, and since its cultural context was well understood by his audience, he chose not to expound on some of the important nuances. Let's try to fill in a few blanks, as we join Jesus as He passed through Jericho on His way to Jerusalem for the last time.

> Jesus entered Jericho and was passing through. And there was a man called by the name of Zaccheus; he was a chief tax collector and he was rich. Zaccheus was trying to see who Jesus was, and he was unable due to the crowd, because he was short in stature. So he ran on ahead and climbed up a sycamore tree in order to see Him, because He was about to pass through that way. And when Jesus came to the place, He looked up and said to him, "Zaccheus, hurry and come down, for today I must stay at your house." And he hurried and came down, and received Him joyfully. When

the people saw this, they all *began* to complain, saying, "He has gone in to be the guest of a man who is a sinner!" But Zaccheus stopped and said to the Lord, "Behold, Lord, half of my possessions I am giving to the poor, and if I have extorted anything from anyone, I am giving back four times as much." And Jesus said to him, "Today salvation has come to this house, because he, too, is a son of Abraham. For the Son of Man has come to seek and to save that which was lost" (Luke 19:1–10).

Uncovering Some Finer Points

Luke shared three key details about Zaccheus to help us better understand the story. He was a "chief tax collector," "rich," and "small in stature." Each of these specifics played a role in the development of the account and how Zaccheus should be viewed. This short Jewish man had won the right to gather taxes for the Roman government in the lucrative trade area of Jericho.[10] While collecting the required taxes, the Romans allowed the publicans (tax collectors) to keep any extra money they could extract from their taxpaying victims. On one occasion, some tax collectors came to John the Baptist to be baptized and asked, "Teacher, what are we do?" (Luke 3:12). John's response was noteworthy, because it sheds some light on the profession's shady practices. He told them what a life of repentance would consist of for them, "Collect no more than what you have been ordered to" (Luke 3:13). Extortion appeared not to be above most publicans' scruples.

In no uncertain terms, Zaccheus was hated by his countrymen for choosing such a livelihood. Not only was he deemed a traitor for collecting taxes to help fund an occupying army, he became wealthy off the backs of his fellow Jews while performing his duties. By lumping in this dubious profession with "sinners," we need to hear the utter contempt ring out from the Jews, when they spitefully used the phrase, "tax collectors and sinners" (ref. Matthew 11:19; Mark 2:16). Not only was Zaccheus a hated publican, but he was also the "chief" of them — odious to the extreme.

Zaccheus's wealth was certainly mentioned to intensify the deep hatred that was felt for the little man, but it also served to draw a correlation to a dangling question that came up earlier on Jesus' trek to Jerusalem. Previously, He had discussed with the rich young ruler (Luke 18:18–27), what it would take for him to "inherit eternal life" (v. 18). After the young ruler assured Jesus that he had kept the great commandments from his youth, he was consumed with brokenness in his heart toward the poor, and the Lord detected it. The young man left Jesus' presence "grieving" (Matthew 19:22) because of his spiritually unhealthy attachment to his possessions over those in need. Confounded by Jesus' disparaging remarks concerning the fate of the rich, His disciples asked, "And so who can be saved?" (Luke 18:26). A question that the story of Zaccheus will address.

Although Zaccheus's "wee" stature brings an alluring charm to the story, it also carries a serious undercurrent. Hate for Zaccheus surely spread into the streets on the day Jesus entered Jericho. Lined up along the road that Jesus traveled, the Jews eagerly desired to catch a glimpse of this lauded religious figure of their day. Zaccheus also fervently sought to see this man who attracted so many followers. However, Jericho's prejudiced populace had no intentions of letting this vertically challenged tax collector up front to see Jesus. Like me, some of you are reasonably tall and have probably allowed someone shorter to stand in front of you to view some event. On that day in Jericho, hate ruled out such kindness. Doubtless, Zaccheus only experienced rudeness and ridicule, as he was pushed aside and unable to initially see Jesus.

Today, do we ever keep others from seeing Jesus? Does our judgment against another's lifestyle or appearance keep them from our Lord? Do others see grace and compassion in our behaviors or legalism and coldness? Do guests at our church services feel a cold indifference to their presence or a warmhearted welcoming? Do we care about the plight of others or do our words of concern result in inaction? Do others see Jesus in us? Years back, a disheveled man visited our congregation wearing a T-shirt with a large alcohol beverage logo smack-dab in the middle of his chest. It was not long before one of our "gospel police" read him the "riot act" about wearing such an inappropriate garment in our place of righteousness. Regrettably, we never saw this man again. Of course, patience is a virtue, and it was sorely needed in that situation. With some acceptance and teaching, I am sure this man would have figured things out in due time. Instead, we placed a roadblock to Jesus in his path. As Christians, one of our roles should be to create pathways to our Lord and Savior. Never, never block anyone from Jesus . . . too much is at stake.

A Dispirited Life and Seeking Jesus
Zaccheus's choice of professions had an oppressive influence on his day-to-day existence. Pursuing riches at the cost of others came with a price. Even with all his money and possessions, he basically had nothing. Life was lifeless. Life was depressing. Hate intruded on almost every aspect of his activities in Jericho. He had heard every disparaging word his countrymen could hurl at him. He was unwelcome at the synagogue, unwelcome at social gatherings, unwelcome in the marketplace . . . just unwelcome! His selfish venture produced loneliness and sadness. Perhaps his servants paid attention to him, but they had no other alternative. Assuming his wealth came through extorting and cheating others out of money, as was typical of the trade, he lived in the constancy of sin. With his spiritual brokenness as well, life was miserable on so many fronts. Could anything or anyone turn his dismal existence around?

At this point, we may want to ask, *Why did Zaccheus want to see Jesus?* Was it just idle curiosity? Had he heard of His many miracles and was hoping to witness one? Perhaps, he had heard of some of His remarkable teachings and wanted to hear His words of wisdom firsthand. Possibly, he caught wind that this righteous Man actually shared meals with other "tax collectors and sinners," and maybe, just maybe, He would entertain dining with him. It's possible that Zaccheus knew Matthew and was aware that he left the lucrative trade of tax collecting to become a disciple of Jesus.[11] If so, you can imagine Zaccheus's tension-filled thoughts: *Would this Jesus take interest in me? Would He talk cordially with me or hurl abuses at me like the rest of the Jews? Maybe He would take the time to share some vital spiritual insights with me. I feel lost and hurt so much . . . yes, perhaps the risk is worth it. I need to go climb that tree!*

A Welcomed Perspective

Scorn-filled words may still have reached Zaccheus as he sat on his perch in a sycamore-fig tree, but the crowd could no longer keep him from seeing Jesus. As Jesus approached the short man's lofty vantage point, the most extraordinary thing occurred, Jesus looked up and made contact with the tax collector's sad, yet hopeful eyes. Already in shock, Zaccheus's shock was only compounded when Jesus invited Himself to dinner and an overnight stay at his home. He hurled no abuses; Jesus simply took interest in the hated publican and spoke kindly to him. Well, we might say that Zaccheus was "tickled pink," as he wasted no time and "hurried" down the tree and "received Him gladly" (v. 6).

In verse 3, we read that Zaccheus was "trying to see" Jesus, or alternately translated, he "sought to see" (ref. NKJV). Never in his dreams did this demoralized tax collector think that he would encounter the ultimate Seeker — "For the Son of Man Has come to seek and save that which was lost" (v. 10). "The" Seeker sought this lost seeker, and He beheld this disheartened man with a caring look.

Luke gave us a direct glimpse of the Jews' hatred toward Zaccheus, as they grumbled about Jesus' desire to stay at the home of a "sinner" (v. 7). I. Howard Marshall states that "to stay in such a person's home was tantamount to sharing in his sin."[12] To the Jews, "outrageous" only begins to describe Jesus' desire to spend time with this societal outcast.

Some recent research may help us better understand how the Jews truly viewed the tax collectors. In a joint neuroscience and psychology study at Princeton University, two researchers examined the neural signatures of its participants while looking at photographs of individuals from eight separate social groups. Each picture was evaluated to determine which of four emotions (pride, pity, envy, or disgust) was elicited the most by the image. Activity in the medial prefrontal cortex of the brain is typically expected when humans encounter one another (even in the case of pictures), so they closely monitored this area during the study. However, the results showed the lack of this neural response when disgust was elicited, as the participants viewed pictures of the homeless and drug addicts. Their results suggest that when we view others with disgust that we dehumanize them. We view them as an object versus another human being.[13]

It's likely that Zaccheus was a victim of dehumanization because of the Jews' extreme hatred toward him. From their perspective, he was lost and should stay that way. He deserved to be thrown out with the garbage and forgotten. Fortunately, Jesus came to save the lost, not ignore them. He saw Zaccheus as a person of value, worthy of his time and care. He had the power and ability to address his spiritual ills and was more than willing to spend some quality time with him.

As I passed through our family room recently, a particular political figure stood boldly at a microphone espousing some distorted claims on a TV news show. To be honest, I stopped and looked at this person with disgust and repugnance. These negative emotions left me in a disturbed state; not because of the person's opinions, it was my view of them as an individual. Personally, I do not want to view others with such animosity. Regarding them as misguided would have been a more constructive way to view such a person. Sometimes we need to ask ourselves do we truly believe in this: "For God so loved the world, that He gave His only Son, so that everyone who believes in Him will not perish, but have eternal life" (John 3:16). Note the "everyone!" I believe that God has put great potential in all of us, yet sin can leave some deep scars. So, I prayed for this individual . . . and myself. Let's save those feelings of disgust for things, not people.

"Seeing" Results

Luke does not give us all the details of what occurred at Zaccheus's home, but undoubtedly, Jesus shared some pivotal teachings aimed directly at the tax collector's brokenness. When Jesus explained the parable of the sower to His disciples, He made the following comment about the seed that fell on thorny grown.

> And others are the ones sown with seed among the thorns; these are the ones who have heard the word, but the worries of the world, and the deceitfulness of wealth, and the desires for other things enter and choke the word, and it becomes unfruitful (Mark 4:18–19).

Jesus probably shared similar truths with Zaccheus. Deceived by the belief that happiness and contentment resulted from the accumulation of wealth and possessions, Zaccheus's passions centered on these unhealthy pursuits. His eyes only saw what pleased him, instead of the people around him who were in great need. Spiritual blindness overtook him, and true life was choked out of him. Zaccheus's eyes only saw Zaccheus and what he selfishly wanted. Jesus opened his eyes to these truths.

Jesus' words fell on a receptive heart that day. Convicted of his shortcomings, Zaccheus stood up and disclosed his repentance by declaring, "Behold, Lord, half of my possessions I will give to the poor, and if I have defrauded anyone of anything, I will give back four times as much." Jesus was now his Lord, not just a lauded rabbi. His eyes were opened to the plight of the poor, as he resolved to commit half his wealth to helping meet the needs of those stricken by poverty. Perhaps, he had defrauded no one, but I believe the context leads us to another conclusion. Zaccheus needed the other half of his riches to pay back all those he had defrauded. Fleecing others was just what tax collectors did in that day. That's one of the reasons he was hated and called a "sinner." Whatever the case, Jesus launched Zaccheus's life on a new trajectory — one of righteousness and eyes that were wide open to the needs of others.

Perplexed by the earlier question to the law-abiding rich young ruler about who can be saved, through the Zaccheus story, Jesus revealed how this can occur. Yes, the truth still exists that "it is easier for a camel to go through the eye of a needle, than for a rich person to enter the kingdom of God" (Luke 18:25). Nevertheless, Jesus left them with this to muse over after the rich young ruler left, "The things that are impossible with people are possible with God" (Luke 18:27). God intervened with Zaccheus through Jesus' action. A seeking heart open to the message of Jesus became enlivened. Surely his followers were astounded when Jesus made the following announcement concerning this rich and hated tax collector; "Today salvation has come to this house, because he, too, is a son of Abraham" (Luke 19:9). Jesus' teachings can produce a remarkable faith, the faith of Abraham. Yes, all things are possible through our gracious God.

We need to develop Jesus' caring eyes for the lost. Personally speaking, I have always felt that I've fallen short in this regard. Having caring eyes toward "tax collectors," (insert who you may) that's hard stuff! I tend to study the Bible with people I am comfortable, and even under those circumstances, those relationships often suffer. I have basically lost friends and been permanently avoided by others with whom I asked to share the gospel. Nevertheless, I genuinely cared about them and deeply desired to bring Christ into their lives.

Years ago, I implored a friend to let me study the Bible with him. He knew I was a busy person, and I was, so he did not want to burden me with another activity. I pleaded with him that this was an important endeavor, and I could make the time. He still would not hear of it, but then he said, "Mike, people have loved me for various reasons, but you are the only person who loves my soul." Yes, he got it. We need to be lovers of souls and let God work through us in that regard. I do believe — with God, all things are possible!

Even with the loss of some friends, the gaining of others as brothers and sisters in Christ has made it all worthwhile to me. Helping to bring others to Christ stands as some of the more important and rewarding undertakings in my life. Tears of joy are the result, and you just want to jubilantly sing the words from the old hymn with them that go — "Glory, Glory Christ is mine, Christ is mine! All to Him, I now resign. I have been redeemed!"

ILLUMINATING THOUGHTS

I've felt that we often desire uniformity in our churches rather than unity. Not only do we impose that on ourselves, newcomers need to be like us: look like us, talk like us, act like us. Differences may upset the apple cart and threaten our equilibrium. Do we really trust God to bring about a marvelous unity out of diversity? One of my minister colleagues, who has an innate love for the lost, told me that his experience bears this out. He noted that individuals whose sins fall out of the norm of his congregation's experience will likely be avoided by his brothers and sisters. Rather than seeing the need for Christ in the lives of such people, his leadership has been reluctant to reach out to them. Concerns about whether they will steal or ask others for money stand in the forefront of their minds rather than how Christ may change their lives and benefit the kingdom. Concerns about how church culture might be impacted has also driven their decisions on how to carry out evangelism. Jesus cared about Zaccheus. We need to care about the Zaccheuses of our society. Yes, things may change. Yes, it may be a little uncomfortable at times. But Christ hung on the cross for them, just as much as He did for us. Perhaps, it isn't culture that needs to change, but our hearts.

Unlike the Jews in Jericho, we must never exclude anyone or give up on them. God is patient for "all" of us to come to repentance (2 Peter 3:9), so we need to exhibit this quality as well. Let's have the eyes of Jesus and see the lost, care about their condition, and come alongside them to help address their hurts and spiritual shortcomings.

Luke also left us with some practical lessons about seeking the lost from the Zaccheus story. First, we should become aware of what affects our "seeing." These perspectives may cause us to exclude others. Jesus saw Zaccheus as lost and cared about his spiritual state. Second, truly take interest in others. Do not let your inquiries just serve as a cold segue way to share God's Word with them, but genuinely take an interest in them and care about their well-being. Third, use kindness when dealing with others. Graciousness opens doors to many people. Fourth, create a relationship over a meal. Few things broach communication like sharing a meal with someone. The resulting relationship may blossom into an opportunity to share the good news with them at some point. Fifth, share the words of life. We never need to be judgmental with others when we share God's Word. Just let those words of life flow and let them do their work. Do we truly believe that God's Word is sharper than a two-edged sword, when it comes to dealing with the heart and intentions (Hebrews 4:12)? Jesus' words had convicting power with Zaccheus and changed him for an eternity. Last, open pathways to Jesus. Through our behaviors, words, openness, and caring, let others see Jesus in us. Caring people created pathways to help us find Jesus; let's do the same for others.

A 'Short' Story

QUESTIONS

1. What is the relationship between "seeing" and the heart? How might you make your "seeing" a little more like Christ's?

2. How did the Jews in the story view Zaccheus? Why and in what ways was this exhibited? How might their view of him have impacted his daily life?

3. Why do you believe Zaccheus wanted to see Jesus? What may have precipitated this?

4. How did Jesus treat Zaccheus? Why did Jesus choose to lodge at his house? How did the Jews view Him for that? What was significant about Zaccheus's proclamation? Is there a Zaccheus in your life to whom you need to reach out?

5. What is the difference between uniformity and unity? How might the desire for uniformity be detrimental to a congregation?

6. What are a couple of practical lessons in the Zaccheus story, and how might you incorporate them in your approach with others?

CHAPTER THREE

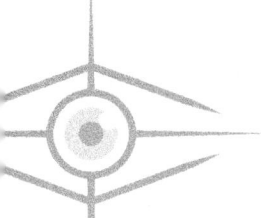

BLIND-SIGHTED

For he who lacks these qualities is blind or short-sighted, having forgotten his purification from his former sins
—2 Peter 1:9.

John Glenn's return to space was at hand. Approximately 36 years had passed since he soared into Earth orbit aboard the Friendship 7 Mercury capsule. Now a sitting senator from Ohio, the 77-year-old astronaut would participate in some aging experiments aboard the Space Shuttle Discovery. Several supportive senators decided to make their way to KSC to witness Glenn's momentous liftoff. Prior to the launch, one of my NASA colleagues and I escorted those senators on a tour of some of the Shuttle's facilities, where they could get an up-close view of one of the Space Shuttles being prepared for a future launch. This was not the "50¢" tour; it was the "million-dollar" version. Never before had I been involved with such a privileged tour. They observed things that most could only imagine. Following the tour, we dropped them off at the viewing area to watch the launch.

Immediately after liftoff, we ushered the senators back to the bus that took them to their cars. As they disembarked at the parking area,

47

each senator had to walk by us, as my colleague and I stood by our seats at the front of the bus. Shockingly, not one of them took the time to offer thanks. They just walked right past us.

Not long after Glenn's mission, the launch of the first element of the International Space Station aboard a Space Shuttle had arrived. Again, my cohort and I were tasked with touring a delegation of individuals from Europe. As I recall, most of them were dignitaries from the European Space Agency, along with a few politicians. We followed much the same routine as we had for the senators, though the tour was not as grandiose. Yet, when this group disembarked and walked past us at the conclusion of the day, their response was different — expressions of gratitude overflowed from each of them.

Why the difference? What made one group more grateful than the other? I believe the senators had an attitude of entitlement and perhaps were distracted by their busy schedules. They were blind to the efforts of their exhausted tour guides by neglecting to express a simple thanks. To be honest, I was not expecting anything but was stunned by their lack of gratitude. Rather than fellow human beings, we were apparently viewed as objects that facilitated their day's adventure and fulfilled their expectations. Basking in their self-deluding light of importance, these senators had become blind to the good deeds of those around them.

SEEING, BUT NOT SEEN

Many physical conditions can cause us to experience temporary blindness. When darkness falls, we succumb to a common human limitation — without the aid of light, moving about in our world can be quite hazardous. If you have ever driven into a dense fog bank, you have learned that driving in such conditions exposes you to the risk of rear-ending another vehicle or having someone plow into you. Our world consists of many obstructions that block or obscure our vision. So, even though our eyesight may be totally functional, these external qualities limit our ability to see. Nevertheless, it is unlikely that these conditions will impact how we perceive others. As we can observe in the aforementioned story, physical obstructions, darkness, and environmental factors are not the only things that cause blindness.

Sometimes we physically "see" others, but our brains virtually ignore their presence. This occurs to such an extent that you may not recall seeing someone at an event, even though you physically saw them. Our focus, interests, and prejudices may have caused us not to perceive them. We noted in the last chapter how Zaccheus's pursuit of wealth had likely blinded him to the struggles of the poor around him. Since they could not help him achieve his prosperous goals, he probably disregarded their presence and walked right past them without seeing their needs.

Sometimes we may innocently fail to pay attention to others and have nothing personally against them. For instance, I knew a young man who was desperately in love with a woman who had been dating another guy for many years. I once asked him, "Why don't you start dating other women, as she may never break up with her long-term boyfriend." He looked me right in the eyes and replied, "She is worth waiting on, so I'm going to stick it out." He literally paid no attention to other women, because he was deeply in love with this woman of his dreams. Virtually, he was blind to the flirting and advances of other women. By the way, his hopeful longing finally paid off, and he married his dream girl.

I collect old science fiction items that predate *Star Trek* and *Star Wars*. I love the way the artists envisioned human space flight before we actually started sending people into space. My eyes are now trained to look for these types of specific collectibles. The features, shapes, artistic design, and colors of these sci-fi gems guide my eyes to fix on such finds. I may see thousands of other items while in an antique store, but most of them go unnoticed because of my single-mindedness of purpose.

Ignoring categories of antiques is one thing, but when our minds choose to disregard others categorically, "we may have a problem, Houston." Unfortunately, our brains can become trained not to see certain individuals for various negative reasons, such as, their appearance, behavior, ethnicity, past missteps in life, or differences from ourselves. We look past them or misperceive something about them, "believing" they are not worthy of our time. We truly need to embrace the fact that God does not wish "for any to perish" (2 Peter 3:9). As His ambassadors for the gospel, much is at stake in helping bring others to Christ, facilitating their healing, and nurturing them to stay the course. Treating individuals like they are a rock alongside a path only serves to dishearten them. With compassion as our guide, we probably all need to rethink how we view and treat others who enter our lives.

When it comes to how societal and religious norms impact one's perception of another person, John gave us one of the most insightful stories. Physical and spiritual blindness are intricately interwoven, where corrupted worldviews and morality lead different groups of characters to victimize an innocent person. Let's turn to John 9 and investigate some eye-opening lessons that will aid in the godly development of our spiritual sight.

'THE LIGHT' BRINGS SIGHT

Jesus was introduced in the prologue of the Gospel of John, as ". . . the true Light which, coming into the world, enlightens every man" (John 1:9). Jesus as the light that illuminates the hearts of people and exposes spiritual darkness was a major theme in John's Gospel. No story better conveys this than the one that describes when Jesus healed the man who was born blind in John 9. Depending on how you slice things, the narrative contains about seven scenes that take place in a relatively short period of time. Our approach will not consist of evaluating all the nuances of the scenes and story but will appraise how the different groups and individuals view, and thus treat, the blind man. Nevertheless, some of the details will be investigated when they contribute to our goals.

To set the stage, Jesus and His disciples came across a blind beggar, probably, in the vicinity of one of the Temple gates that would allow him to plead for alms at a main thoroughfare. Jesus healed him of blindness, setting in motion a series of short vignettes. Physically, the former blind man took center stage in the discussions that followed. Jesus was the central figure of the dialogue, even though He does not appear again until the end of the story. Let's now dissect how the characters viewed the blind man, which precipitated their behaviors. We will not always follow a chronological order, if it aids in our evaluation.

The Disciples' View

The disciples only made a bit appearance in the story, but their question to Jesus, concerning the man who was born blind, served to identify some shameful accusations and subtle undercurrents that propel the story forward. They asked, "Rabbi, who sinned, this man or his parents, that he would be born blind?" (v. 2). Note that their explicit question left no room for an alternative, which revealed their beliefs concerning the man's blindness. Like most Jews of their day, the disciples believed that such a disability was a punishment levied by God for a specific sin. Either, the man sinned in his mother's womb, or his parents sinned before the birth.[14] This interpretation led to their view of the blind man. He was the manifestation of sin, and his current state was warranted. As these notions drove their woeful perception, the disciples viewed the lowly man as an opportunity for a theological debate, not someone whose suffering should be addressed. Blinded by their beliefs, they held no compassion toward this blind man. He was just one of life's conundrums.

Possibly still in earshot of the blind man, the disciples asked their piercing question. He had probably heard these accusations before, nevertheless, the resulting pain surely continued to run deep. If you ever experienced a barbed attack concerning some aspect of your appearance or a disability that you endure daily, the hurt can be devastating, even debilitating. Believing he was cursed by God, many of the Jews likely walked by this man every day with total disregard or shot a reproachful glance his way. Yet, there always seems to be those few whose arrogant boldness propels their scorn just a little further, and they verbally remind such a man of his "loathsome" state.[15]

As you might have imagined, Jesus provided them an unexpected alternative — "*It was* neither *that* this man sinned, nor his parents; but *it was* so that the works of God might be displayed in him" (v. 3). In essence, Jesus said (my words), "This man's affliction is not to demonstrate God's justice, but His compassion." Even though the disciples' accusative question may not have been mean-spirited, it was directed at an innocent man. The disciples' understanding aligned with that of the Pharisees (v. 34), and in this story, that was not a good thing.

Jesus then boldly said, "I am the Light" (v. 5). "The Light" then illuminated the blind man's eyes and physically healed him. Undoubtedly, Jesus had a secondary purpose in mind for His kind deed. His disciples' eyes were devoid of compassion toward the man, so their judgmental attitudes needed to be exposed. His response and subsequent action accomplished that. They needed "the Light" as well, but in their case, to address their spiritual eyes.

After Jesus' death, John and Peter encountered a man lame from birth at one of the Temple's gates (sound a little familiar). While they gazed into the man's eyes, Peter said,

> Look at us . . . I do not have silver and gold, but what I do have I give to you: In the name of Jesus Christ the Nazarene, walk!
> (Acts 3:4,6)

No disregard or indifference toward the lame man occurred in this incident. They didn't just heal him; they graciously gave him their full attention while doing so. Not only did the former lame man "walk" into the Temple with the two Apostles, but he leapt for joy and praised God for all to hear. Mission accomplished — "viewing" issue cured!

Years ago, I was fervently preparing to teach a class on angels. At that time, the number of sound books on these mysterious beings was surprisingly limited. I remember reading a particular book, when I came across a controversial subject. I believed that the author's approach to this difficult topic was nothing short of outlandish. Personally, I thought he was a "loon," and whatever he wrote was not worth reading. Without hesitation, I quit reading his book and did not pick it up again for another 20 years.

While attending the Harding School of Theology several years later, I developed a love for certain scholars. I started buying their commentaries and books, whenever I could find them at a bargain price online. One day, while reading one of the commentaries by one of my favorite scholars, I noticed that his book addressed that same controversial topic. I became dumbfounded as he proceeded to develop the same position as "the loon." This time, I continued reading and did further research on the topic by other scholars. My whole opinion on the matter changed. My perception of the author that I formerly disregarded quickly changed, and I am still ashamed of my impulsive, smug response to someone who dealt appropriately with a topic.

I've changed my opinion on many biblical topics through the years. Your experience has probably been like my own. Knowing this should impart a certain amount of humility in each of us — none of us have it all figured out! I've seen such horrible conduct by "Christians" toward one another over differing opinions of Scripture. For example, I've seen heated arguments, mean-spirited personal attacks, loss of friendships, divisive behavior, and slanderous speech. You've probably seen similar behavior. Let's learn to respect one another's opinions. Let's discuss issues with open Bibles and prayers for guidance rather than impulsive, heated debates. Let patience and graciousness rule your time together. Never be a know-it-all, because you don't, in fact, know it all! And if you continue to disagree with someone over time, still love one another. That's what Christians do.

The Neighbors' View

Jesus fashioned some mud from His own spittle and applied it to the blind man's eyes (v. 6). He then asked him to go wash in the pool of Siloam (v.7). For the first time in the blind man's life, light poured into his eyes as the water rinsed the mud away. The beauty of a blue sky and green trees flooded his vision. While observing people milling about and quizzically staring his way, joy surely overtook this blessed man. As he most likely returned to the place where he encountered his Healer, some of his neighbors and other acquaintances (whom we will collectively refer to as neighbors) took note of him. An important question for our study is, how did John portray these neighbors? Is it a positive or negative portrayal? And how has their view affected their behaviors toward the former blind man? Some scholars believe the neighbors should be viewed in a positive light[16], but I believe an investigation of several aspects involving the neighbors will demonstrate otherwise. As we examine these features, I will also point out how they affected their view of the former blind man.

First, none of the neighbors rejoiced over the man's astounding good fortune. You would think they would be happy for him, and the tone of this scene would be celebratory. Instead, an air of suspicion seemed to drive their disbelief and questioning. Second, these so-called neighbors never call him by his name. He was not Isaac. He was not Benjamin's son. They "saw him as a beggar" and referred to him as "the one who used to sit and beg" (v. 8). That certainly isn't an endearing title from one's neighbor or a fellow synagogue member. A blind man relied on begging to survive during this time frame in Palestine. So many of the Jews would have given him alms, since the Law required them to take care of the poverty-stricken. Nevertheless, this man's need to beg would come with the stigma that his condition was caused by sin. As such, he would be viewed with disfavor. By designating him as a "beggar," rather than using a more congenial title, the neighbors levied a negative assessment against the former blind man.[17]

Third, the neighbors could not collectively agree whether this cured man was the one who was formerly blind. Yes, he probably looked a little different with his eyes open and a smile on his face. Nevertheless, this man had never been treated as a human being because of his condition. They had walked by him in total disregard for a long time, so why would they know his features or the sound of his voice? So, for his neighbors and fellow synagogue members to argue over his identity was reprehensible. John's portrayal of this surely should not be viewed in a positive light.

Fourth, John revealed a foundational piece of information to the overall story in verse 14 — the healing took place on the Sabbath. Obviously, these Jewish neighbors were, indeed, aware of what day it was. Therefore, as the former blind man explained the succinct details of his healing, they would have recognized Jesus' curative mud-making and its application as "forbidden work" (per Pharisaic traditions). And walking to the pool of Siloam and washing? You got it: "work" again. To these legalistic neighbors, Jesus and the former blind man had both broken the Sabbath. With all that "exhausting" work (sarcasm of course), these "fine" neighbors felt the only appropriate thing to do was to take the man to be grilled by their Pharisaic leaders. Not an overly loving approach for one's neighbors to take.

Fifth, after the parents came before the Pharisees, John revealed a little more pertinent information that may have influenced the neighbors' behavior — ". . . for the Jews had already reached the decision that if anyone confessed Him to be Christ, he was to be excommunicated from the synagogue" (v. 22). When the former blind man mentioned that Jesus was responsible for the healing (v.11), the alarms probably started going off in their fear-plagued craniums. No one confessed anything, but certainly, "such business" with this Jesus needed reporting. Therefore, they wasted no time in bringing the man to the Pharisees to have a memorable conversation about it.

Last, after hearing of Jesus' involvement, the neighbors immediately asked, "Where is He?" At first glance, such an inquiry may have been just a curiosity. However, recognizing that the Jews previously stood ready to stone Jesus for blasphemy in the Temple grounds (8:59), the neighbors' desire to speedily know of His whereabouts appears suspicious and likely contributed to their decision to take the former blind man to the Pharisees.[18]

If we truly embraced loving our neighbor as ourselves (Leviticus 19:18; Matthew 22:39), a natural consequence would be to rejoice with them, when good things come their way. Two millennia later, my heart still breaks for the anonymous blind man. Where was the celebration? A monumental miracle took place! The eyes of a man born blind were opened. The remarkable gift of sight flooded his world. That's a reason to rejoice, not barrage someone with questions and skepticism. Paul asks us to "rejoice with those who rejoice" (Romans 12:15). God's people should genuinely experience delight for another person's good fortune. I've seen the destructive results of envy my whole life. It can produce disharmony and destroy relationships. Most of us have, at some point, allowed this vice to control our thinking and conduct. Another enemy to rejoicing with others is indifference. We just "don't give a hoot." If we are to "love one another" (John 13:34), as Jesus asks, we need to care about how the events of life impact them. Rejoicing demonstrates our care, and perhaps, it will reinforce the efforts that resulted in their life's blessing. Recognize the presence of these two traits and be determined to allow God to help you eliminate them. As I like to think of it, offer up some fertile ground for God's Spirit to do His transformative work. This will allow us to "see" others like Jesus saw them.

The Parents' View

Not trusting the former blind man's initial testimony, the Pharisees summoned his parents. To them, a ruse must have been in the works, and his parents needed to reveal the truth. You can imagine their reasoning: "The neighbors might be fooled as to his identity, but his parents won't." "He may not always have been blind, or maybe never." "This Jesus is a 'Sabbath-breaker,' so this 'sinner' could not have performed such a remarkable sign." "Perhaps, this whole thing is an elaborate hoax." [19]

Blinded by their legalism, these jaded leaders sought three pieces of information from the parents to expose this possible ruse. Whether he was their son, the parents admitted that he was and disclosed that he was born blind. But when asked, "Then how does he now see?" (v. 19), an evasive reply came back at the Pharisees.

> ... but how he now sees, we do not know; or who opened his eyes, we do not know. Ask him; he is of age, he will speak for himself (v. 21).

That isn't the response we might have expected from loving parents. They left their son "high and dry" to defend himself against these misguided bullies. Most certainly, the parents knew a miracle had occurred. It's hard to believe that they did not know that Jesus had cured their son, especially when they volunteered the information that they did not know "who opened his eyes." By adding such a comment, they successfully evaded any questions concerning Jesus. After hearing his parents' response, I can imagine that the son probably hung his head in sadness and disbelief. What motivated these parents to abandon their son? John injected the following note to help us understand the circumstances.

> His parents said this because they were afraid of the Jews; for the Jews had already agreed that if anyone confessed Him to be Christ, he was to be put out of the synagogue. For this reason his parents said, "He is of age; ask him" (vv. 22–23).

Fear fashioned their response. Unlike a disfellowship from a church today, to be put out of the synagogue meant religious and social ostracism, which would likely lead to their financial ruin. Today, we could join another church, but of the dozens of synagogues in first-century Jerusalem, banishment from all of them was the result. This was a daunting matter for the parents, so they abandoned their son to the mercy of the unmerciful.[20]

One thing bothers me about these parents, so I am going to speculate a little. My parents would have never deserted me in a time of need. I called one of my sisters, and she totally agreed with me. She added, "that our mother could be a bear, when one of us was at risk or threatened in some way." I know the former blind man's parents faced a possibly formidable outcome, but to desert their son seems excessive. So, perhaps something else contributed to their actions.

As was mentioned earlier, the common belief of the day for the man's blindness from birth was that either the parents sinned or their son sinned in the womb. Surely, the parents knew they had not sinned, so they must have believed that their son was to blame. From their perspective, he justly suffered at the hands of God. Nevertheless, they had surely endured a lot of scorn and unpleasant glances from their fellow Jews through the years. I am not saying that they did not love their son, but they possibly felt that their misfortunes had gone on long enough. So, they drew a line in the sand and would not enter the fray any further. Their son was on his own.

What specifically did this "line in the sand" entail? John shared with us the following passage that sheds some light on the overall situation involving Jesus.

> Nevertheless many, even of the rulers, believed in Him, but because of the Pharisees they were not confessing *Him*, so that they would not be excommunicated from the synagogue; for they loved the approval of people rather than the approval of God (John 12:42–43).

The Pharisees institutionalized their misguided beliefs in such a powerful way that it resulted in most of their fellow Jews loving the "approval of people" over the "approval of God." The parents' desire for the approval of their leaders, and inclusion in synagogue life, came at the expense of their son— regrettably, a sad reality that did not go unnoticed by him. Rather than celebrating with others, he stood alone to face the intimidating tactics of the Pharisees.

The Pharisees' View

Not unexpectedly, the Pharisees dealt with the former blind man in a fairly despicable manner. The only reason I use the descriptor *fairly* is because some of the Pharisees initially thought that he might be telling the truth. They viewed the healing as a remarkable sign that could not be performed by a sinner (Sabbath-breaker) (v. 16). However, they either changed their viewpoint or were intimidated by their peers, because such an opinion did not surface again as the story proceeded. Personally, I believe they were likely called out by their spiritually blind brethren. There was a reason Nicodemus came to Jesus by the cover of night (3:2). He was later looked on with contempt by the Council, when he suggested that Jesus deserved due process (7:50–52). John described Joseph of Arimathea (a Councilmember, Luke 23:50), as a "secret" disciple of Jesus "for fear of the Jews" (19:38). Obviously, any possible association or showing favor to Jesus could leave one in a precarious position.

Let's look at how the former blind man interacted with the Pharisees through his eyes. Probably still overjoyed to have gained his eyesight, they greeted him with more questioning and skepticism. He must have wondered, *Cannot anyone be happy for me?" "This Jesus miraculously cured my blindness! Why are they arguing over what He did, don't they trust what I just told them? Why question my parents about my former condition... they really don't trust me! Until today, I had never seen a Pharisee, but what I am seeing is pretty revolting.*

After the Pharisees finished questioning the parents, they started to badger the former blind man again. They believed the truth of the matter had not been told and asked pointedly, "Give glory to God; we know that this man is a sinner" (v. 24). Don't misunderstand, by asking for him to "give glory to God," they were not prompting him to praise God for the miracle. They did not trust his testimony and were directing him to glorify God by telling the truth.[21] He never wavered from the truth and continued to provide them with it, as he eloquently exclaimed,

> Whether He is a sinner, I do not know; one thing I do know, that though I was blind, now I see (v.25).

Spiritually speaking, the former blind man's eyes were opening more and more to the light of Jesus, while the Pharisees' sight continued to dim due to their unbending adherence to their errant rules. In our life's course, let's always help open the eyes of others to Jesus, not close them.

When the Pharisees asked him to repeat how he received his sight, things started to heat up (v. 26). Realizing that they did not trust his story and were probably trying to entrap him in some inconsistency, the former blind man became irritated with their interrogative games. He then queried them, "... why do you want to hear *it* again? You do not want to become His disciples too, do you?" (v. 27). Wow, under the circumstances, those were "fighting words."

After they reviled him, the former blind man used some of their own teachings against them. He may have been blind all those years in synagogue, but he was listening. He countered with sound theological logic by saying:

> Well, here is the amazing thing, that you do not know where He is from, and *yet* He opened my eyes! We know that God does not hear sinners; but if someone is God-fearing and does His will, He listens to him. Since the beginning of time it has never been heard that anyone opened the eyes of a person born blind. If this man were not from God, He could do nothing (v. 30–33).

Through all this negativity, God was still at work. All the questioning allowed the former blind man to deeply reflect on the day's events, and he started to realize that there was something incredibly special about this Jesus. At first, His healer was "the *man* who is called Jesus" (v. 11, italics added for emphasis). He then professed that Jesus was "a prophet" (v. 17). Lastly, he declared that He was "from God" (v. 33). And while staring down these egotistical legalists, the man articulately defended Jesus with a sound theological assessment.

Viewing him with utter contempt, the Pharisees spewed their spiteful venom back at him: "You were born entirely in sins, and *yet* you are teaching us?" (v. 34). They were wrong on both accounts, but too blind to see. They unjustly and cruelly put him out of the synagogue. Sometimes, even today, defending Jesus comes with consequences, but we must remain gracious and stick to the truth.

Alone and ostracized from his people, this anonymous man faced a difficult road ahead. What should have been the happiest day of his life took a horrible turn for the worst. Or did it? Likely at his wits' end, the former blind man may have sat and mused over the sad turn of events — *I only did what the man of God told me . . . I so wanted the gift of sight. I only told the truth. My neighbors looked at me with skepticism. My parents left me to fend for myself against the Pharisees. I followed the Pharisee's teachings, and my theological assessment was sound. What did I do that was so wrong to deserve this? Does anybody care about me?*

Yes, Someone did.

Jesus' View

Perhaps, my favorite part of this story dealt with a subtle detail. Moved by his compassion, Jesus gave the man born blind the gift of eyesight. That's a phenomenal miracle and act of kindness, but not my favorite part. Some of the former blind man's responses to the Pharisees were extremely sharp-witted and enlightening, but none of those rose to the top. When the blind man confessed that Jesus was the Son of Man, that was certainly fantastic and warmed my heart, but no, still not my favorite. What I loved most involved Jesus' return to the story. When He heard that the man He healed had been tragically put out of the synagogue, Jesus took the time to seek him out. Fear did not control Jesus' action . . . care did!

Jesus' concern for the former blind man opened the door to share His identity. He did not revile, disregard, treat scornfully, or look down on him. He chose to be in his presence and valued him. This encouraged the man to eagerly listen to Jesus. When Jesus queried him about the Son of Man, he desired to know who He was, so he could believe in Him. Jesus avowed that He Himself was the Son of Man. As the man's spiritual eyes were dramatically opened, He made an earnest confession of faith — "'I believe, Lord.' And he worshiped Him" (v. 38). Jesus not only gave him physical sight, but spiritual sight as well.

Like Jesus, we need to take notice and value others. And in their times of despair, we need to do what we can to lift them up. Obviously, we need to respect people's wishes to be alone and understand that they may not be willing to let us too close after certain events. Nevertheless, at times, the right words from the right person may totally change their outlook and demeanor. I've had this happen a few times in my life and will forever be grateful to those friends who took the time to raise my spirit and renew my confidence. One time the individual had no idea that I was hurting, but their Spirit-led words of encouragement made me realize that God's fingerprints were all over my endeavors, so I weathered the storm and stayed the course.

Showing that you genuinely care, and I mean *genuinely*, may open future doors to share the gospel. In our me-first society, one of the most useful evangelistic tools we possess is the ability to take notice of someone's dire needs and sacrificially reach out to them. Performing such a good deed conveys that we truly care about "them." Seeing Jesus in us may create a desire in them to know more about what makes us tick. So be ready to share the source of your love, and how He lives through and sees you with the Father's eyes. May we all have our Father's eyes!

ILLUMINATING THOUGHTS

Most of us have disregarded a particular segment of our society at some point in our lives. Not in a disparaging way, but as we encountered someone with special needs, an uncomfortable fear overtook us. This discomfort produced a desire to avoid the situation and person. When we struggle to relate, we just do not know what to do or say. Differences from ourselves, in any regard, often trouble us when dealing with others, but especially ones of this nature. Our sneakers cannot remove us fast enough from such circumstances. When my mother went into a nursing home, I had a similar reaction to the elderly in that facility. Hospitals tend to bring on such feelings as well. I would like to share a story to close out this chapter that may help us deal with these fears.

After the Pathfinder spacecraft landed on Mars, our Center Director at KSC asked me to chair a think tank. Our charter was to come up with a strategy for our Center's potential involvement in future human Mars missions. In the early stages of this effort, a woman named Karen approached me about adding her to this august team. She had an interesting skill set and appeared to be an out-of-the-box thinker, so I welcomed her aboard. Karen and I became great friends through the years, and I came to know her on a personal and deeper level. From the outset, she displayed a remarkable sense of humility and gentleness. Though, it did not take long for me to realize that those traits worked harmoniously with a powerful inner strength that produced an admirable assertiveness. She was not aggressive, just humbly assertive. Jesus probably dealt with most people in such a manner, and as I later realized, Karen strove to live by a Jesus-centered code of ethics.

Before I met Karen, she had worked for a research company in Austin, Texas, where she had met her future husband. He had flown in from Florida to make a presentation. Not only was she attracted by his physical appearance, but his intellect also appealed to her. They hit it off and started a long-distance relationship. After about a year, things started to turn serious. Before things went any further, he wanted Karen to meet his two-year-old daughter. She was aware that the little girl had a severe case of quadriplegia, but he recognized that Karen needed to see firsthand the severity of her condition. Obviously, Karen's involvement with her care could have far-reaching impacts on her life.

As Karen anxiously awaited their arrival in the airport terminal, she beheld Annette for the first time. Tucked into a carrier, the little girl was lying in a fetal position. Her face and body were grievously disfigured from her horrible malady. Karen was asked to use great care in touching Annette, as her distorted skeletal system produced severe muscle pain if she was not handled correctly. Such a first impression would have scared me to death. However, Karen immediately realized "how much this little girl needed her." Amazingly, it was love at first sight.

The scary part for Karen did not involve the daunting aspects of Annette's care but in leaving her beloved state of Texas and transitioning to a new job in Florida. She eventually made her way to Orlando, where her fiancé lived, so she could start helping with Annette. She worked at nearby KSC, mostly with NASA, for the rest of her career. This former valedictorian came to realize that she would need to sacrifice her PhD dreams to help with the overwhelming requirements of Annette's care. "Overwhelming" is not an exaggeration, as many surgeries followed to rebuild her hips, release her spastic muscles, straighten her spine, bring functionality to her hands, and alleviate her pain. Physical therapy was utilized to bring tone to her muscles, especially to help normalize her facial features and allow her to hold up her head. These procedures were interspersed with trips to the emergency room to combat seizures, and the cries of pain from various activities, like the simple task of changing a diaper.

Prayer brought comfort to Karen along the way, because she knew God had prepared her for such a nurturing responsibility. From early in life, Karen cared about those with special needs and who faced various challenges in life. In second grade, she befriended a mentally disadvantaged classmate with whom others would not associate. In fifth grade, she made friends with and supported her preacher's daughter who lived with Down's Syndrome. Later, at a children's home, she tutored and helped the children with their homework. While in college, she taught at a daycare for welfare children. This was no easy task, as some had never even held a crayon. And one child even tragically witnessed their mother being shot in the leg by the father. Yes, God had been preparing Karen.

Along the way, Annette started improving, and some of her medications were stopped. Her personality started to come out, and she became more expressive. Karen could not help falling deeply in love with this sweet little girl. In fact, Karen stated that this child not only "enriched her life but taught her a depth of love that she would not have otherwise known." Their bond became so deep-seated that she developed a dependency on Annette's love and presence, as she pines for her, when they are apart.

Karen told me that Annette is quite smart, can interact with others, and enjoys attention. Unfortunately, they have experienced the worst in people, when they encounter Annette. For example, parents have quickly snatched their children away from her presence, as if they would catch something. She is completely disregarded at times, and sadly, Annette can detect that as well.

Karen provided some general advice from her experience of working with special needs children through the years. Talking to their parents first is typically a good idea to learn how to best communicate and interact with each child. Most certainly, learning how to help the parents of a special needs child is extremely beneficial. Like anyone else, she would like her daughter befriended, talked to, loved on, and kindly greeted. Annette can sense the love from others, and like all of us, dearly desires it.

Yes, reaching out to some folks may be intimidating at times, but our inclusive and loving God wants us to be inclusive and loving as well. God's love flows freely to all, so perhaps it's time that you let yours flow freely too.

QUESTIONS

1. How does Jesus demonstrate that He is the Light in the story of John 9?

2. How did Jesus' disciples view the blind man? Did Jesus view him in the same manner? Explain the differences, and what did Jesus do to correct His disciples' vision.

3. What do you think John was trying to convey in his description of the neighbors' response to the blind man's gift of sight? What drove their actions? How would you expect a true neighbor to respond?

4. What inner trait shaped the parents' answers to the Pharisees' questions? What did their answers communicate to their son? How would you have answered their questions?

5. How did the Pharisees view the former blind man? What kind of response did they get from him? Were there judgments blinded by anything? Explain.

6. What should we take away from how Jesus viewed and treated the blind man? Reflect on how you might need to improve how you "see" some specific individuals?

CHAPTER FOUR

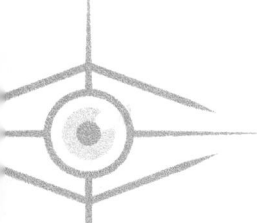

SYMPATHETIC EYES

... God of all comfort, who comforts us in all our affliction so that we will be able to comfort those who are in any affliction with the comfort with which we ourselves are comforted by God
—2 Corinthians 1:3–4.

Standing by the jumping pit with a rake in my hand, I watched my son sprint down the running lane. After effectively executing the triple jump's required hop, bound, and jump phases, he went airborne and created a deep cavity as his feet hit the loose sand. As the judge stretched out the tape to measure the length of the jump, I knew my son had come up a little short of his typical mark. Unfortunately, he had contracted an intestinal virus and did not have the energy to perform up to his usual standards. The previous year, he had gone to the high school state championship in the triple jump, and given that his numbers had continued to improve, I felt he would easily qualify again for that honor at this year's regional meet.

I had just finished raking the pit, and when I looked up, I saw my son preparing to make his final jump. He looked drained. The sickness had robbed him of his normal youthful vigor. For the first time, a dreadful feeling came over me. I suddenly realized that this jump would likely be the last time that I would ever see one of my children perform in a competitive event of this nature. My daughter's high school soccer team competed in three regional finals and the state championship one year. Because she was now away at college, I knew that this jump would likely bring to a close my fun-filled journey of memorable sports moments with my children. My son gave it his all, but the jump came up short. With it, an era of my life had come to a close.

What happened over the next several days took me by surprise; anytime I was alone, I could not hold back the tears. A somber mood and strange hurt enveloped me. A part of my life that I loved dearly had come to a sad end, leaving a gaping void. Grief inexplicably possessed me. As we all go through life, we come to learn that death is not the only life-loss that can elicit grief. Life-losses come in many different forms, such as the loss of a job, broken relationships, retirement, moving, graduation, loss of a pet, becoming "empty-nesters," loss of health and youthful vigor, miscarriages, and divorces. We should be cognizant when others are going through such times and be empathetic to their plight.

SYMPATHY, A DIRE NEED AND CHRISTIAN TRAIT

Psalm 69 describes a man in horrible distress who needed help. Metaphorically, he described his circumstances as if he were helplessly sinking in a mucky bog and on the verge of drowning in flood waters (v. 2). His very life was at risk. What brought about his dire situation? His list was ominous. He was hated without cause and the target of destruction by powerful enemies (v. 4), falsely accused (v. 4), persecuted for religious zeal (v. 7, 9, and 11), alienated from his family (v. 8), the object of gossip, and humiliated in the songs of drunkards (v. 12). The resulting reproach, shame, and dishonor prompted by his adversaries had left him emotionally and physically destitute (v. 3 and 20). He longed for someone to come alongside him to help ease his relentless burdens. Did a caring neighbor, understanding countryman, or spiritual friend come to his aide? Here was his take on the situation.

> Reproach has broken my heart and I am so sick. And I looked for sympathy, but there was none; and for comforters, but I found none. They also gave me gall for my food and for my thirst they gave me vinegar to drink (v. 20–21).

The therapeutic value of sharing his troubles with a sympathizing friend did not occur.[22] The soothing comfort from someone who cared about him never came to fruition. In fact, instead of gaining some much-needed support, more pain and suffering was brought his way (from the metaphor of the food and drink given him).[23] Alone, disheartened, and exhausted, this man tearfully carried a burdensome load.

God's people should never be indifferent to the plight of a brother or sister. Obviously, we cannot all run to someone's side during difficult times, but we can do a few things. Peter shared the following with his readers:

> To sum up, all of you be harmonious, sympathetic, loving, compassionate, and humble (1 Peter 3:8).

Peter appeared to be addressing the character traits necessary for the development of healthy relationships among Christians that would, in turn, allow their churches to flourish. Of course, the trait of expressing sympathy applies to our relationships outside our churches, as well. What is Peter specifically asking of us? In one regard, he desires for us to "enter into and experience the feelings of another."[24] Immersing ourselves in the emotions of others can be tricky business, but it will allow us to extend support as well. Paul also desired Christians to extend sympathy to one another as can be seen in the following appeals to the churches in Rome and Corinth.

> Rejoice with those who rejoice, and weep with those who weep (Romans 12:15).

> And if one part of the body suffers, all the parts suffer with it; if a part is honored, all the parts rejoice with it (1 Corinthians 12:26).

Such support of one another goes a long way in producing harmony and brotherly love. Sympathy is an expression of compassion, which, in turn, expresses itself in behaviors of comfort, consolation, understanding, and support, along with a sharing in someone's distress.

Our familiarity with the experiences of others can help us sympathetically enter their situations, because it gives us some level of understanding of what they may be experiencing. Typically, suffering alongside someone may be needed in some circumstances. Our sympathetic response may come through an understanding of why they may hold such a strong position over a matter of opinion. For example, having a glass of wine with dinner may be viewed differently by someone who was raised by an abusive, alcoholic parent. As we consider how to approach such a matter, addressing this individual sympathetically versus running roughshod over their views, will allow us to more sensitively handle the subject.

The Greek term for "sympathetic" also has a "practical bent" — as we understand and participate in the feelings of a fellow Christian, we should provide the appropriate assistance when necessary.[25] Driven by compassion, the acts of sympathy flow from a caring heart and not a matter of obligation. The author of Hebrews provided an excellent example of this when he commended his audience for standing firm and supporting one another during past persecutions (Hebrews 10:32–34). He specifically praised that they had "shown sympathy" toward those who had been unjustly imprisoned (v. 34).

Though fraught with inherent concerns, these compassionate souls did not steer clear of ministering to their brothers and sisters in prison. Often in ancient times, those imprisoned required others to bring them food and other necessities.[26] For example, Paul appealed to Timothy to bring his tunic, while he was in a Roman prison, probably due to the onset of winter (2 Timothy 4:13). Jesus also lauded the sympathetic act of visiting a brother in prison and stated that it was like they had done this very thing for Himself (Matthew 25:35–40). Such behaviors encompass the life of the righteous and lead to eternal life (Matthew 25:46).

Perhaps most of all, we should take great comfort in the fact that Jesus fully sympathizes with our weaknesses in the face of temptation (Hebrews 4:15). We can all relate to the intense pressure that temptation yields. Even though, we often fall to its insidious weight, Jesus, in all His humanity, never did. He took on its full, enticing force without succumbing to it. Remember, biblical sympathizing goes "beyond the sharing of feelings" and should include a component of help when necessary.[27] So how does help come about relative to a sympathizing Jesus? Help is available at the throne of God through our prayers (Hebrews 4:16). Jesus opened our access to the throne. He is there at God's right hand. He intercedes for us there (Romans 8:34). He, like no other, understands and sympathizes with our human frailty in relation to temptation. As the writer of Hebrews basically stated, confidence, not timidity, should then embody our prayers.

> Therefore let's approach the throne of grace with confidence, so that we may receive mercy and find grace for help at the time of our need (Hebrews 4:16).

Considering the context, "help at the time of our need" would definitely include assistance in the face of temptation. Our great Sympathizer is there to attest to our need.

Let's turn to a story in which Jesus "sees" the devastating results of grief in the lives of beloved friends.

A STORY OF LOVE AND SYMPATHY

A few of my colleagues at KSC loved to answer their coworkers with the following joy-filled statement when asked about how things were going, "It's a great day at the rocket ranch." And so, it typically was. Nevertheless, like in any walk of life, joy can shift to grief like the flip of a switch. Early in my career, one of our high-energy officemates tragically died in a car wreck. The rocket ranch was at peace one morning until someone broke the news that this well-liked engineer had died in a head-on collision the night before. That engineer was destined to have a great career, but none of that mattered anymore. Our friend and colleague was gone, and our daily camaraderie was replaced with disbelief and agonizing grief.

Nobody escapes the piercing talons of grief in this life. Some people may hide their grief well, while others are public with their painful emotions. Most of us are also quite lost when entering a grief-stricken environment. We wonder what to say and do. Circumstances often dictate our response. Such things as our relationship with the suffering individual and the timing of a visit can make a huge difference. Also, grief manifests itself in people in different ways. Its pace can also vary. The coming pages are not meant to be an end-all in how to deal with such situations. Many books in the marketplace are well-suited for providing advice on how to handle grief, but hopefully, the story presented in John 11, along with some of my personal examples, will provide you with some ideas on how to sympathetically navigate these waters a little better. John 11 is typically remembered and admired for Jesus' ultimate miracle in the raising of Lazarus from the dead. However, this story also contains a lot of human drama from which we can learn much. Lazarus's two sisters were left behind after his death, and John shared how Jesus handled two different but delicate encounters with them.

We do not know how long Lazarus had been sick, but a turn for the worse obviously prompted Mary and Martha to send for Jesus (John 11). They surely realized that death loomed over their brother, since they were willing to take Jesus away from His ministry. John included two noteworthy statements that carried an important theme forward in this story.

> So the sisters sent *word* to Him, saying, "Lord, behold, he whom You love is sick" (v. 3).

> Now Jesus loved Martha and her sister, and Lazarus (v. 5).

They were not just acquaintances or good friends . . . they were beloved friends. Jesus knew that Lazarus would die and that He would raise him from the dead to glorify God and Himself (v. 4). This benevolent act would lead many to believe in Him (v. 42, 45). Nevertheless, because of Jesus' love for Mary and Martha, a concern for their emotional well-being surely started to trouble Him. He was aware of the human condition and how grief could ravage even the strongest person over the death of a loved one. He knew entering the grief of these two beloved friends would be difficult.

Mary's Outpouring of Grief

Let's jump ahead in the story to when Jesus encountered Mary, but first we need to become familiar with a few pertinent details. Jesus had delayed making His trip to Bethany for a couple days (v. 6), so when He arrived, Lazarus was already dead and entombed for four days (v. 17). Prior to meeting with Mary, Jesus had a private conversation with Martha (we'll come back to that scene in a moment). Jewish mourners had come to the sisters' home (v. 19, 31) to console them. Let's pick up with the moving scene that involved Mary, as Martha left Jesus' side.

> . . . she left and called Mary her sister, saying secretly, "The Teacher is here and is calling for you." And when she heard *this*, she got up quickly and came to Him. Now Jesus had not yet come into the village, but was still at the place where Martha met Him. Then the Jews who were with her in the house and were consoling her, when they saw that Mary had gotten up quickly and left, they followed her, thinking that she was going to the tomb to weep there. So when Mary came *to the place* where Jesus was, she saw Him and fell at His feet, saying to Him, "Lord, if You had been here, my brother would not have died." Therefore when Jesus saw her weeping, and the Jews who came with her *also* weeping, He was deeply moved in spirit and was troubled, and He said, "Where have you laid him?" They said to Him, "Lord, come and see." Jesus wept. So the Jews were saying, "See how He loved him!" (John 11:28–36).

After Martha discreetly let Mary know that Jesus wanted to see her, she quickly made her way to Him just outside Bethany (v. 28–30). The mourners assumed that Mary had headed to the tomb to "weep" over her brother, so their concern for her prompted them to follow her (v. 31).

As Mary approached Jesus, what do you think He "saw?" Were her eyes red and puffy from crying? Did she look exhausted? Were lines of stress noticeable on her face? Did she look like "normal" Mary? Personally, I believe that Jesus saw a person stricken by the debilitating power of grief. Jesus' concern for her would not only have been heightened, but likely, His own emotions started to stir as well.

Holding Jesus in high regard, Mary fell at His feet and said, "Lord, if You had been here, my brother would not have died" (v. 32).

Most certainly, her faith in Jesus' healing power was evident in those words. Nonetheless, considering her emotional state, her tone probably gave away her grief-stricken disappointment. Right after uttering those words of sorrow, Jesus "saw" her crying (v. 33). Her tender heart was laid bare before the Lord (ref. John 12:3). Those difficult words of her brother's death probably became strained as grief's intensity came on her with all its force, and she could hold back her tears no longer. The Greek conveys that her crying was an unrestrained wailing. Her mourning friends were deeply moved by her sorrowful outburst and joined in with their own chorus of loud crying.

At my mother's celebration of life, I remember walking out of our church's auditorium at the end of the service. I desperately wanted to refrain from crying, as we paraded past our dear friends who came that day. Their sympathetic eyes were fixed on us. While walking next to my daughter, I made the mistake of making eye contact with a good friend. And guess what? Their eyes were filled with tears. I could not handle it. I immediately burst into tears and gently laid my head against my daughter's beautiful blonde hair, crying the rest of the way to the back. I know that I too easily wear my emotions on my sleeve. I have often said that "I would cry because Wile E. Coyote did not catch the Road Runner and would not have dinner that night." Tears flow easily in my family and hold a contagious power over most of us.

At such an incredibly sad scene involving someone you deeply love, Jesus naturally became "deeply moved in spirit and was troubled" (v. 33). With His human emotions now deeply aroused, Jesus asked, "Where have you laid him" (v. 34). With loud crying just seconds before, the mourners' response was surely laden with quivering and choked up voices. They replied, "Lord, come and see" (v. 34). Jesus' emotions were no longer just aroused but engaged, as John shared that "Jesus wept" ("wept" here being a quiet sobbing) (v. 35). God's

Son wept. "The Word" who "was God" wept (John 1:1). "The Word," whom "all things came into being," wept (John 1:3). "The Word" who "became flesh" wept (John 1:14). The depth of Jesus' humanity was on display. Sympathetic eyes led Him to join Mary in her grief and cry at her side. That's what she needed — tears of a sympathizing Savior. Not empty platitudes, not a sermon, not advice nor a Bible verse. What she needed at this moment was for Jesus to step into her grief and cry with her. So He did. The mourners were partially right when they saw Jesus crying and exclaimed, "See how He loved him!" Yes, He loved Lazarus, but Jesus knew He would raise him and see him again. The tears were a sympathetic outpouring from Jesus' soul for Mary, as she agonized over the death of her beloved brother.

Some scholars suggest that the word translated as "deeply moved in spirit" denotes a spirit of anger. For instance, Jesus became angry over the power of death in the world or that Mary and the Jews crying exhibited a lack of faith in Him. Even though such an interpretation is possible, it virtually holds the word in isolation. The basic context and movement of the passage provide no support for such an interpretation. Anger is just not present in this scene, and to the contrary, the passage exudes the deep concern for a beloved friend, as He sympathetically hurts for Mary. Love is a thematic element throughout the whole story. Collen M. Conway points out that when this word is "used to describe an internal attitude, as in our case, it may indicate more generally a deeply felt emotion."[28] The preferred interpretation should be that Jesus was moved by Mary and the mourners' grief, and He sympathetically responded by sobbing with them. The New American Standard version that we are using does an excellent job of translating this word, which allows for the proper interpretation of this passage.

The above is important, because of what The Epistle to the Hebrews shares with us concerning Jesus.

And He is the radiance of His glory and the exact representation of His nature, and upholds all things by the word of His power (Hebrews 1:3a).

Jesus revealed the nature of His Father to us (see also 2 Corinthians 4:4, 6). He is the "exact representation" of that nature. Exact! That nature (or image) is the goal of our transformation journey from one glory to the next (2 Corinthians 3:18). We need to understand our God's nature, and where we fall short of it, so we can partner with the Holy Spirit to press on to that image. Through this scene of Jesus and Mary, we can truly appreciate the sympathetic nature of our God. So, when you reflect on who God is, understand that when His people hurt, He hurts along with them . . . to the point of tears.

Let me share with you a few stories from my life that may help you in developing sympathetic eyes in times of death and loss. Walking within the hurt of others is not an easy task, and most of us will never fully master it. Hopefully, these stories will help you to sympathetically travel through similar tumultuous waters.

My father's funeral was wholly conducted at his grave site. I am not sure why we chose that approach, but it seemed appropriate at the time. Several of my friends from KSC attended the service. None of them knew my dad, they just wanted to support me in some way. As I mentioned earlier, I cry easily, and that day was full of tears. After the service was over, many of those in attendance lined up to share their condolences. I'll never forget the sharing of grief that occurred with one of my co-workers. As he approached me, his eyes cautiously met mine. He then uncontrollably burst into tears, and his face started to redden. His words were consoling, as he gave me a hug, but his sympathetic eyes and tears are what deeply touched me. I knew him to be quite a serious individual who was stoic in his demeanor. For him to have such a sympathetic outburst of emotion toward me was extremely meaningful— perhaps, more so than anything else that occurred that day. I cannot remember the words that he shared, but I can vividly still see his facial expression 25 years later. He truly stepped into my grief and shared in my sorrow. It was genuine. It had therapeutic power. Strangely, I can only remember one other person's face that day, and yes, that person was also crying.

Another sympathetic moment that had great significance to me occurred at my mother's viewing. It transpired over a short period of time. It involved no words, no hugs, and involved no tears. A dear friend from my church used to love visiting my mother in her assisted-living facility. They talked casually for a while, and then he liked to read to her some select passages from the Bible. He told me that his visits were designed to encourage her, but he was the one who walked away encouraged. My mother was gifted in that way. When she passed away, I remember dreading participating in the viewing. In hindsight, though, one precious moment turned that event into a cherished memory for me. On the evening of the viewing, which was well-attended, I was distracted by all the sympathizers and the stories that they shared. For some reason, while I was standing beside my mother's casket, I looked across the room. There, standing next to the wall by himself, I saw my mother's reader. He did not make his way toward me; he just made eye contact with me. That was all he could do. His sympathizing gaze spoke volumes. He communicated a depth of caring that I would not have believed possible. Wow! Sympathy's healing power flooded my very soul. I would not trade that moment for the world.

Lastly, several years ago, a good friend's dearly loved son died in a high-speed traffic accident. Alcohol-induced road rage took this 18-year-old young man's life way too early. My friend and his wife were devastated. My wife and I were at our wits' end trying to determine what to do. We took food to their home to help ease their burden, especially since many people were coming into the area for the funeral. After the memorial service, as they were trying to carry on with life, I told my wife, Carol, about an idea that I had come across in my studies at the Harding School of Theology. Living memorials have a way of helping people process grief, so my idea was to plant an oak tree on their property in honor of their son. After asking their permission, we planted a tree for them in their son's memory.

When this young man was a child, he had trouble saying the word *moccasin*. In a childlike way, he simplified this awkward word and said "moskin." His parents loved telling stories about him calling water snakes "moskins." I can still see and hear them laughing, as they shared those precious memories. So, when we planted this beautiful live oak in a spot where they would see it every day, we hung a sign on it titled, "The Moskin Tree." As you might imagine, they were moved by this gesture and extremely grateful. Before long, they added a bench under the branches of the tree.

Almost a decade went by, and I wondered if that tree turned out to be meaningful to them. It had grown into a gorgeous tree and majestically adorned the approach to their house. With the bench at its base, it provided a serene setting. I wondered, though, if it helped them process their grief. I asked my friend if that was the case. He said, "Absolutely!" These were some of the comments he shared...

- "Sitting on the bench, under that tree, became a sanctuary for me."
- "While reflecting there, I stepped through my son's entire life."

For him, this sacred space had become a place of "good thoughts" and "prayer." Thankfully, it turned out to be a wonderful expression of sympathy and support.

Perhaps planting a tree is not a way that you would choose to remember someone, but you can honor one's memory in other ways. I have left books in libraries in honor of someone. Two families at my church recently erected benches on the church grounds in memory of their parents. You can dedicate an area of a garden to a loved one who has passed on. Some people create scholarships in a family member's name. Things that continue to give something back in some way are what you might want to consider. These types of deeds might not help everyone; but for many, it can help them constructively process their sorrow.

What About Martha?

You're probably asking yourself, *Why is there talk about Martha in a chapter about sympathy?* Unlike the scene with Mary, no flow of emotions was apparent in the text. It's not that they were non-existent, but the emotional states of Martha and Jesus were not John's primary interest. In the scene with Mary, Jesus' humanity was clearly evident. To the contrary, Jesus spoke authoritatively with Martha, as deity, as the Son of God. Judge for yourself:

> ... Martha, when she heard that Jesus was coming, went to meet Him, but Mary stayed in the house. Martha then said to Jesus, "Lord, if You had been here, my brother would not have died. Even now I know that whatever You ask of God, God will give You." Jesus said to her, "Your brother will rise *from the dead*." Martha said to Him, "I know that he will rise in the resurrection on the last day." Jesus said to her, "I am the resurrection and the life; the one who believes in Me will live, even if he dies, and everyone who lives and believes in Me will never die. Do you believe this?" She said to Him, "Yes, Lord; I have come to believe that You are the Christ, the Son of God, *and* He who comes into the world" (John 11:20–27).

Some scholars see a pointed rebuke or mild chiding in Martha's words to Jesus because of His delay. Others detect grief and sadness over the whole matter. To be honest, her attitude is not clear. However, I think it's safe to say that Martha was grieving. Most likely, despair peppered with disappointment fueled the tone in her voice, since Jesus had not arrived in time to heal her brother. Like Mary, her words exhibited faith that Jesus had the ability to heal Lazarus. Martha's initial statement was identical to what Mary had said but was probably delivered in a much different tenor. Perhaps, the two sisters used these words over the previous few days to bemoan the fact of the dreadful consequence of Jesus' delay. "If only" is a familiar qualifier for most of us in times of sorrow.

John and Luke tend to present Martha as a common sense, practical, and frank person (ref. Luke 10:38–42; John 12:2). So perhaps her words to Jesus display her grief-driven disappointment laced in a cold stark reality of the situation. Her subsequent statement expressed her continued confidence in Jesus' power despite her brother's unfortunate death.[29]

Can we interpret Jesus' subsequent discussion with Martha as sympathy? Wholeheartedly, yes! Crying often dictates a sympathetic approach with someone, but the lack of it does not negate such a response. Mary *needed* Jesus to cry with her. Martha did not. Her grief required a different sympathetic act to address her need.[30]

To Martha's ears, Jesus' opening response would have just sounded like the common belief of the day amongst the Pharisaic Jews that her brother would rise again. Those were words she had probably heard many times over the last several days from the Jewish mourners. Jesus may have alluded to His upcoming miracle in this comment, but Martha did not interpret it that way. In fact, nowhere does she appear to predict such an outcome (ref. v. 39).

Jesus detected a core matter-of-faith issue in the heart of Martha. She needed to move past the abstract faith of the resurrection to a personal trust in Him. Not only was the power of resurrection at His beck and call, but He was the "resurrection and life." Her faith in an abstract concept of resurrection only brought a vague hope. A personal faith in the One who would accomplish it could lead to a tangible, living hope. Jesus sympathetically gave Martha what she needed. Passionately believing in her Savior's words, Martha wholeheartedly embraced this truth in her confession. She found a new hope for an eternal life with her brother through her personalized belief in Jesus.

I would like to share a word of warning. In times of crisis, such as after the death of a loved one, it is rarely appropriate to swoop into a grief-stricken situation and give much advice. Being present, listening, and letting them cry will be the best courses of action. There may be some rare instances when advice might be helpful to clear up a matter for someone to aid the progression of their grief. Walk carefully here; we are *not* Jesus.

ILLUMINATING THOUGHTS

I would like to leave you with three diverse stories that do not involve the loss of a close relative, friend, or beloved church member. These will not only allow you to see the role sympathy plays in these other areas of life, but hopefully, will spur some ideas of your own for situations you may face.

From Misfortunate to Fortunate

Several years ago, a well-liked deacon at my church went forward during the invitation. He was well-liked because he was a true servant of God, loved God, loved others, and was a remarkable Southern gentleman. He's just one of those individuals that the more you get to know him, the more you fall in love with him. When he went up to the microphone to share what was on his heart, he could hardly get a word out before the tears started to flow. He emotionally explained that his company had decided to make some changes, and he had unexpectedly lost his job. This placed his family in a difficult financial situation. His only appeal was for prayers that he could find a way through these difficult times. As I remember, our pulpit minister came up and put his arms around him and shared a little more of the story. He told us that his daughter was getting ready to go off to college and that they had just purchased a new home. But another little-known item was that his benevolence had further aggravated the situation. For some time, he had been studying the Bible with an impoverished man and his wife. His heart went out to the circumstances they faced, and he started to financially support them, which complicated his current situation. What our preacher did next caught us all off guard. He asked the ushers to bring the offering baskets to the front and asked the congregation to give as their hearts moved them. People scurried to write checks and pull money from their wallets and purses, as the baskets were passed around. As you might imagine, our deacon was genuinely humbled at the gesture, and then he started to cry. The whole scene was extremely moving.

Later, I learned that the congregation donated several thousand dollars. In a church of just a couple hundred members, that was quite a sum of money for an impromptu request. I cannot speak for anyone else, but my giving in this situation was an act of sympathy and a privilege. I just know it was a needful act for a beloved brother. Sympathy sometimes works in remarkable ways.

Max the Cat

The following is a social media post that I wrote a couple years ago in a therapeutic attempt to ease my emotional pain. I have included several sympathetic comments I received from some of my friends, a few of whom I had not seen since high school. I was caught off guard when 74 of my friends took the time to comment on my post. Without a doubt, some of my friends chose to sympathetically enter my suffering by writing some of the most meaningful words, attempting to ease my pain. Online venues provide us with a powerful means to extend sympathy to others.

It was not supposed to happen that way. About 15 years ago, my daughter and wife summoned me around midnight to help rescue my daughter's cat, MoMo, from the middle of a dense thicket of palmettoes. MoMo had escaped the safe confines of our home earlier that day and had not returned. He appeared to be making a sound like he was injured, so into the palmettoes I went with a flashlight in hand. Of course, with the poisonous snakes we have in Florida, such a venture in the middle of the night was reckless at best. Sure enough, once I was deep into this hard-to-navigate *Florida flora, I heard this muted "meow." I cleared away some of the palm fronds and saw the cat . . . he just was not ours. Very lean and leery of us, he was probably dumped on our property by someone. My wife begged to keep him, as she wanted to have a cat that she could call her own. Thus, Max entered our lives. Unfortunately, he stuck to me like glue. He loved me dearly, and my lap has not been my own for 15 years. As he routinely climbed into my lap, he lovingly, though sternly, looked into my eyes as if to say, "Stay still for a while, for I need a nap." Now in about an hour, we are going to take him to be put to sleep. He is suffering greatly, and so am I. I was truly blessed by his life; now I am* grief-stricken *— odd how blessings can result in such pain. Prayers are definitely appreciated.*

> "I am so sorry Mike and Carol . . . they are not just an extension of family . . . they are family . . . God's beautiful creatures whom He entrusted us to care for are the best!! Praying for you and Carol's healing and you all keeping the fun memories of MAX alive in the coming days ahead."

> "My heart is going out to you. A pet is a family member and it hurts so bad to lose one. My eyes are tearing up just thinking about your pain. Max was blessed to have you, and you were doubly blessed to have him. You were a lucky family to have him."
>
> "I lost my tomcat a few months ago. I had bottle fed him from a baby. I miss him so. Definite prayers. I feel your heartache."
>
> "I am so sorry . . . my heart aches for you and Carol. You will always be known in our hearts as Grammie and Poppy Max" [Explanation: Our first grandson differentiated us from his other grandparents by giving me and Carol these titles].
>
> "I'm so sorry, Mike. You know what a cat lover I am, and I know how hard this is for you and Carol. We will pray that your sweet memories will help heal your grief."

I shared these comments, so you could see the depth of sympathy in the words. I believe many of these folks could not express their concern for me without tears running down their face. To be honest, some of these sympathetic messages brought tears to my eyes. I cherished their healing effect, and wow, did I feel the love. Firsthand expressions of sympathy are important when appropriate, but cards and electronic media provide us with wonderful instruments to share our sympathy with one another.

A Friend in Great Pain

Lastly, I would like to share the following short story (with a few minor edits) that I included in my book *Created for Good Deeds*. I think you will find this story beneficial, as it comments on the importance of building good relationships which will help us sympathetically reach out to our friends.

> Building relationships is a personal investment in others. They learn what we believe, and whether our actions are consistent with what we profess. They come to understand whether we care about them or are selfishly motivated. They make a determination whether we can be trusted with their personal information, and if we have the ability to potentially help them. I'll never forget one particular Sunday morning a number of years ago; I was talking with one of my Christian brothers in the foyer of our auditorium before services began. From the corner of my eye, I suddenly saw one of my close friends open the backdoor of the foyer and make a beeline straight for me. As he approached, I noticed he looked disheveled and horribly upset. He immediately pulled me aside and revealed a shocking problem that was consuming him. Ministry was not going to take place that morning by going into the auditorium and listening to a sermon. After just a few minutes, sympathy dictated what I needed to do, so I drove him to a local park, where we could talk in private. He poured his soul out to me for the next hour while crying uncontrollably. Knowing this man like I did, there was no way he would have shared the intimate details of his issue without a deep trust in me. That trust developed over a long period of time, and even then, it took utter desperation for him to reach out to me. It just was not in his make-up to lean on others.[31]

I was able to extend sympathy to my friend that day simply by being present. I pretty much let him pour out his grief while I listened. His hurt went deep. I think I made a comment or two to help him think rationally about the matter, but mostly, I remained silent. Consoling, not counseling, is what he needed.

QUESTIONS

1. What life losses, other than the death of a loved one, have you experienced? Did others reach out to you during those times in meaningful ways? If so, describe. If not, how might you have been comforted by others?

2. Describe what sympathy is. Identify a few acts of sympathy.

3. How did Jesus extend sympathy to Mary (John 11)? Knowing Jesus reveals God's nature to us, what did you learn about God from the scene of Jesus and Mary?

4. Do you believe Jesus extended sympathy to Martha? Explain, and note any results.

5. Give a couple of examples where sympathy can be extended, and it does not involve a life loss. Also, suggest how sympathy may play a role in such circumstances.

6. In Hebrews 4:15–16, in what way does Jesus sympathize with us? Knowing that sympathy can have an element of help, how does this occur?

7. After reading the Max the Cat post in the "Illuminating Thought" section, create a comment that you believe would help an individual deal with the loss of their pet.

CHAPTER FIVE

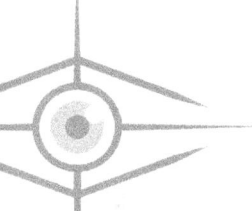

A SHEPHERD'S VIEW

Like a shepherd He will tend His flock,
In His arm He will gather the lambs and carry them in the fold of His robe;
He will gently lead the nursing ewes
—Isaiah 40:11.

From the trailhead, the hike to Hemlock Falls in Northeast Georgia was 0.8 miles. Like most trails to waterfalls, it started out rather flat and smooth, but before long, my wife and I discovered that we needed to step over the many roots and rocks that randomly cluttered the path. Moccasin Creek followed along the trail most of the way. Its crystal clear water afforded an unobstructed view to the rocky bottom and glimmered where the sun snuck through the heavily forested canopy. The creek's serpentine route added to the beauty of the walk. We watched it flow its sinuous journey as water twisted around boulders, made short falls over rock faces, smoothly slid down granite slides, and cascaded down the creek bed. At times, the creek roared as it narrowed or descended rapidly, while at other times, it peacefully flowed along the way. About two-thirds of the way through the hike, the stream made a 90-degree turn, and we came to a narrow bridge with a wooden guardrail on one side. As we crossed this tenuous structure, the water rushed underneath us and then violently went over a 5- to 10-foot waterfall, while making a right turn to follow its original course.

Along the hike, we came across numerous seeps that watered the path. This added to the adventure, as we had to rock-hop through these muddy areas. Also, steep escarpments typically rose up on the side of the path opposite of the stream. Rhododendrons clung to the side of these cliffs, while hardwood trees, such as oaks, hemlocks, and birches, majestically rose up, reaching for the sky all around us.

To adorn our way, some of the mountain's wildflowers had started to bloom. Purples, yellows, and whites decorated the trail's landscape in certain areas. We also came across several small waterfalls along the way that trickled down about 50 foot sheer drop-offs.

Arriving at Hemlock Falls, the forest opened up, revealing the waterfall as it flowed over a 15-foot tall granite face into a beautiful, deep green pool lined by boulders. The creek took an immediate right turn and then back left again creating a slightly turbulent flow over the rock-strewn creek bed. Even though the waterfall was not very tall, the overall scene was breathtaking. We climbed over the boulders directly across from the waterfall and sat on a log that had embedded itself there from a past flood. That was our dining room for lunch. As we ate our sandwiches, we would break off some of the bread, and toss it out in the pool, where rainbow trout would swim up and strike at it. We also tossed bits of bread into some of the trapped water along the rocks to watch for crawdads to come out for a little lunch as well.

Such places are sacred to me. They bring me peace and joy. I find them restorative and enlivening. I clearly see God's fingerprints there. As reflection overtakes me, I praise my glorious God, whose creative majesty and artistic prowess is second to none.

I hope you have found such sacred places. For you, they may exist in a garden, at the beach, or while looking through a microscope or telescope, but wherever they may be found, we need to intentionally encounter God there, marvel at His work, and find rest.

You are probably wondering, *How does this story relate to a shepherd's view or perspective?* Just stay with me, and you will "see."

THE GOOD AND DIVINE SHEPHERD

At times, Jesus used the metaphor of a shepherd to convey His leadership role, relationship to His followers, and certain aspects of His mission. In John 10:1–18, Jesus interpreted Himself in this manner in considerable detail and twice emphatically identified Himself as a shepherd with a heralded "I am" statement.

> I am the good shepherd; the good shepherd lays down His life for the sheep (v. 11).

> I am the good shepherd, and I know My own, and My own know Me, just as the Father knows Me and I know the Father; and I lay down My life for the sheep. (v. 14-15).

Jesus intimately "knows" His sheep, which He compared to His loving relationship with His Father. This "knowing" consists of an understanding that deeply cares about the needs of His sheep to the extent that He would sacrificially give up His life for them.

David used this same metaphor for God in Psalm 23. David not only viewed God as his shepherd, but the first-person language in the psalm appears to indicate his firsthand experience with God's shepherding influence in his life. God knew David. He knew his needs and addressed them appropriately. Let's focus on the first few verses of the psalm and examine some of the roles of the Shepherd conveyed by David.

> The LORD is my shepherd,
> I will not be in need.
> He lets me lie down in green pastures;
> He leads me beside quiet waters.
> He restores my soul;
> He guides me in the paths of righteousness
> For the sake of His name.

With God as his shepherd, David totally trusted Him to sustain, guide, and care for him. David's knowledge of shepherding allowed him to fully understand that God knew him, cared about him, and recognized his needs. Because of this, David could confidently state that he would "not be in need." God's provision for him would be satisfactory for whatever circumstances he encountered in life.

Caring attentiveness is a core ethic that shapes a shepherd's service. In the psalm, the Divine Shepherd obviously observed David's need for rest. The former young shepherd envisioned God leading him to a beautiful green meadow and coaxing him to lie down there.

Let's examine the metaphor a little deeper to better understand what was transpiring. Sheep graze from sunrise to late morning and then have a stomach full of undigested grass. At this point, they need to lie down to rest and chew the cud to start the digestion process. Sheep do not always understand what they need and may be apprehensive about lying down. They need to feel secure and calm to rest well. To lie down for the shepherd, the sheep must not only fully trust him, but they must know his voice to be able to follow his cues. For David, as God led him to the green meadow and prompted him to lie down, he would hear His Master's voice and trustingly follow His guidance (ref. John 10:4). God's voice was one he trusted. It was a voice from the Shepherd who cared about his welfare. David was confident that he would be protected by God during this period of relaxation. Through the years, I've witnessed many people get diagnosed with stress-related illnesses. Perhaps like David, we need to pay attention and trust our Divine Shepherd's prompting and learn to relax in His loving protection.

Next, the Divine Shepherd led David to a tranquil pool of water to address his needs. As you might imagine, sheep are not good swimmers. Waters with turbulent flow make them nervous, and dropping their heads down to drink can make them vulnerable to predators. Under the vigilant eye of the shepherd, David was led to "quiet waters," where he could truly relax and let the water and its serene setting perform its revitalizing work. We know from many stories in the Bible that God can be extremely ominous at times. Yet, these verses remind us of His tender nature toward His sheep.

As we continue into verse three, I believe verse two provides for us the context of David's progression of thoughts. God quieted David's soul and restored his energy while he lay in the peaceful settings of green meadows and quiet waters. God then placed David on the "right" path, one leading to His well-being and blessedness.[32] Even though these verses appear to be primarily dealing with David's psychological and physical welfare, they obviously refer to his spiritual condition as well.

CARING FOR AND GROWING THE FLOCK

As an extension of His ministry, Jesus sent out the apostles in pairs on mission trips (Mark 6:7–14). Mark noted that during their journeys they had preached repentance, cast out demons, and healed the sick (vv. 12–13). Let's pick up with the text after they returned.

> The apostles gathered together with Jesus; and they reported to Him all that they had done and taught. And He said to them, "Come *away* by yourselves to a secluded place and rest a little

while." (For there were many *people* coming and going, and they did not even have time to eat). And they went away in the boat to a secluded place by themselves. *The people* saw them going, and many recognized *them* and ran there together on foot from all the cities, and got there ahead of them. When Jesus went ashore, He saw a large crowd, and He felt compassion for them because they were like sheep without a shepherd; and He began to teach them many things (Mark 6:30–34).

After Jesus listened to the Apostles' report, He observed a disturbing trend. Jesus and His disciples' notoriety had grown into superstar status. Many people continuously sought them out. This had grown to be such a hindrance that they did not have much time to eat a meal or rest long enough to recover from their trips. The Good Shepherd knew He needed to lead His flock to the serenity of "green pastures" and "quiet waters," so he loaded them onto a boat to take them to a secluded place for some alone time.

During the early portion of my career while I worked as an engineer on the Space Shuttle Main Engine's avionics subsystem, there were a few times that we encountered serious problems and had to work a horrendous amount of overtime. I remember one occasion when I had worked 12-hour days, seven days a week for several weeks. With little children and tasks at home, acquiring adequate rest was not possible. I literally daydreamed about sleeping. I desperately yearned for some "quiet waters" to recover.

Shockingly, when Jesus and the apostles landed the boat at the "secluded" place, a needy throng of people besieged them. Expecting solitude, they encountered multitude. How the crowd beat them to their destination is a mystery. Possibly, the boat encountered a headwind, or they steered the boat to a closer isolated cove.[33] Whatever the case, these determined folks quickly decided not to let the apostles escape. They literally ran together to beat them to

A Shepherd's View

their destination. Jesus' planning had gone awry. It looked like their recuperative trip hit a snag.

Personally, I find Jesus' reaction to the crowd stunning. He took His apostles to what was normally a lonely place, yet they were anything but alone. This was not a new group of people. Surely, many of these individuals were responsible for the exasperating problem from the start. Jesus tried to flee their presence, but there they were again. You pick the word: *annoyances, irritants, nuisances* . . . that's basically what they were. Anyone would be justifiably irritated in such circumstances enough to say, "Please, leave us alone and go away; we need some rest!" But not Jesus, He looked on them with "compassion."

Years ago, Carol and I were fortunate to attend a congregation with an active young adult group. We immensely enjoyed participating in that group, appreciating one another's company and doing all kinds of activities together, including camping. On one occasion, about a dozen of us went to the Ocala National Forrest for the weekend and stayed at the Salt Springs Campground. This was a beautiful place with a natural mineral spring and gorgeous, sprawling oaks throughout the camping area. Many of us were looking forward to a lot of good fellowship and escaping from the hustle and bustle of our daily lives.

One young man who went with us was a newcomer to our close-knit group. We were still getting to know him but welcomed him on the trip. He was kind and fun-loving, but a little socially awkward. On the first evening, after eating and a lengthy period of enjoyable fellowship together around a campfire, we realized time had gotten away from us, and it was midnight. Due to the day's busy events, everybody was exhausted. We all headed to our tents for a good night's sleep, except for our new friend and one other individual. They never went to sleep. They stayed up the whole night loudly carrying on and laughing incessantly. Most of the bothersome noise came from the new guy.

Since most of us did not sleep well, we were not in the greatest of moods the next morning. One brother had, what seemed like, a wonderful idea. He suggested that we annoy our new friend throughout the day, so he could not fall asleep before nightfall. Obviously, we wanted him to go to sleep that coming night. After breakfast, our boisterous friend walked over to the other side of the spring to a peaceful spot on a grassy knoll to take a nap. One of the men quickly followed him and greeted the drowsy young man with a nudge and some unwanted conversation. His day continued in similar fashion; we allowed him no sleep before nightfall. Our plan worked. He slept like a baby that night, but he was quite upset with us.

While working on this chapter, I thought again about this incident. In no uncertain terms, his loud behavior that first night was extremely rude. Nevertheless, in all his awkwardness, did he even realize he was being obnoxious? Naïve and oblivious to the needs of others, his intentions were not mean-spirited. My poorly developed eyes at the time could only see him through a lens of irritation and disgust. If I had looked on him with compassion, I might have handled the situation a little better. Perhaps, I could have graciously pulled him aside and let him know how his behavior had adversely affected the rest of us. Dealing with irritating people can challenge our Christian character, especially when we have been victimized by their conduct. A mature Christian approach to this unfortunate episode might have led me to think through the situation a little differently and address my awkward friend with some degree of care. I had quite a bit of maturing ahead of me at the time.

Back to Jesus' reaction, "He saw a large crowd, and He felt compassion for them." What did He actually "see?" Through His perspective, He saw a collection of people that were "like sheep without a shepherd." He looked upon the faces and eyes of this group and knew they desperately needed a leader, especially a spiritual leader. On another occasion, Jesus had a similar response, when He encountered a multitude.

> Seeing the crowds, He felt compassion for them, because they were distressed and downcast, like sheep without a shepherd (Matthew 9:36).

Basically, the religious rulers and teachers of the day had left the Jewish people in a hopeless and spiritually inept state. Rather than nurtured, they were harassed. Rather than offered care, they were bullied. Rather than taught God's truths intertwined with love, they were trained in strict traditionalism, which gave rise to judgmentalism. This resulted in the people feeling downcast and helpless to address their spiritual needs. As the good Shepherd, Jesus knew what He needed to accomplish.[34] They were spiritually starving, so He fed them.

Jesus' compassionate response to the crowd was to teach them. We do not know exactly what, but most likely, it entailed teachings concerning the good news of the kingdom of God (ref. Mk. 1:14–15; Mt. 4:23). According to Mark, the teaching appeared quite lengthy (v. 35), so conceivably, it consisted of much of the material presented in the Sermon on the Mount, including what facilitated the flow of spiritual blessings, how being a light consisted of performing good works, how righteousness involved embracing the essence of the Law with the heart, how they should pray, the need to develop a heart whose treasure was in heaven, and putting aside anxiousness and seeking first the kingdom of God were several of the possible items discussed by Jesus. The Good Shepherd was adding to His flock. His sheep needed to know His teachings to properly follow Him. They needed to unmistakably know His voice.

The wise Shepherd could also use a lengthy period of instruction for a secondary purpose. During Jesus' teaching, the tired 12 could relax and listen. Perhaps, compassion steered Him to judiciously use His time to accomplish a couple of goals.

You may be asking, *I am not a shepherd, nor will I ever be, so how is this relevant to me?* Looking on others with compassion is the starting point. We need to use this trait to ask the question, are the behaviors (or lack thereof) of others potentially related to a lack of training? In our churches, we may note that certain behaviors of our brothers and sisters are unchristian. On an individual case, we may take someone aside and gently show them what God's Word says about one aspect of their conduct. However, when many others seem to exhibit the same problem, perhaps we could recommend to the deacon of the teaching program that offering a particular class might be wise. I remember a woman who struggled with gossiping, but she did not realize that her comments were gossip. She believed that since her remarks were the truth, she wasn't gossiping. Of course, gossip is often true but can be hurtful when certain things are passed to others. Gossip plagues many churches, and we should desire to get our brothers and sisters on the right path and could include a class that educates its attendees on what builds others up versus what tears them down.

Years ago, I detected that there was a need for a class on the Holy Spirit at my congregation. My brothers and sisters just did not understand who He was and what His role is. Moreover, I was disturbed by some of the erroneous teachings concerning the Holy Spirit at the time, so I decided to go to the leadership and request that they let me teach a class on this important subject. They considered it but declined my proposal. To be honest, they were afraid of the topic. A few years later, we were attending another church, and I noted a similar problem. I again asked the leadership of that congregation for permission to teach a class on this subject. They joyfully accepted my offer, so I educated my brothers and sisters on the Holy Spirit for a quarter. At the end of the course, a woman who was close to twice my age approached me, her eyes beaming. She pulled me aside and said, "I never thought someone would teach this old dog new tricks, but you did! Thank you! I just did not properly understand these things." I had a burning passion to teach this topic, which I believe came from a care for my brothers and sisters to truly understand this crucial and formative subject.

Equipping for service is another area worth discussing, so I have devoted the entire "Illuminating Thoughts" section to address this.

Sometimes, new teaching techniques also need to be suggested. I remember when skits were introduced during Vacation Bible School years ago at my church. To kick off the evening's theme, participants performed a short skit to highlight some of the biblical concepts being taught that night. Unfortunately, a small minority were opposed to this and waited in the foyer until the skit was completed. They felt the kids were not attending VBS to be entertained but to learn. They missed an important truth about skits; they are a valuable teaching tool to convey the essence of the biblical stories to the children. Not surprisingly, I still remember some of those skits but remember little else from those VBS weeks.

The bottom line is this: Our teaching programs should be multi-faceted and intentional, not only educating but also providing insights for Christian living, promoting Christian formation, and equipping us for service in various capacities.

ILLUMINATING THOUGHTS

In recent years, I have come to believe that our teaching programs in many congregations often miss an important target. Our Bible class teachers typically do a good job at educating their classes about the Bible and providing us with practical insights. They do a fair job at facilitating spiritual formation through their teaching. However, when it comes to training for service, we tend to come up short. A correct understanding of the Bible is important, but in and of itself, it can make us arrogant (1 Corinthians 8:1), and even judgmental. Knowledge that is embodied and coupled with love (as well as the other Christian traits) allows us to become more like Jesus. Basically, that is the spiritual formation part of teaching. Nevertheless, even spiritual formation can become self-serving if our focus is only inward. As Christ is formed in us, our focus should turn outward. In fact, if the "image of Christ" formed in us does not include an attitude of serving others, that image is likely corrupted or immature in its development. Paul emphasized the outward focus of the Christian walk.

> Do nothing from selfishness or empty conceit, but with humility consider one another as more important than yourselves; do not *merely* look out for your own personal *interests*, but also for the *interests* of others (Philippians 2:3-4).

> For we are His workmanship, created in Christ Jesus for good works, which God prepared beforehand so that we would walk in them (Ephesians 2:10).

> ... who gave Himself for us to redeem us from every lawless deed, and to purify for Himself a people for His own possession, eager for good deeds (Titus 2:14).

With such strong direction to look out for the needs of others and to address them the best we can, our training should help us in this area. Paul specifically made mention of such training to the church in Ephesus.

> And He gave some *as* apostles, some *as* prophets, some *as* evangelists, some *as* pastors and teachers, for the equipping of the saints for the work of ministry, for the building up of the body of Christ; until we all attain to the unity of the faith, and of the knowledge of the Son of God, to a mature man, to the measure of the stature which belongs to the fullness of Christ (Ephesians 4:11-13).

Knowing this to be true, let's be intentional with some of our teaching to equip our membership "for the work of ministry" (or service). I would like for us to examine one minister's story who came to realize how his congregation was lacking in this area and how they addressed it.

For one Central Florida minister, his congregation's approach to living the Christian life seemed amiss. Church attendance numbers were great (and perhaps even considered high for a Florida church). Evangelistic efforts produced several converts. However, many of them did not remain faithful. Even though their weekly attendance was good, the number of individuals involved in serving others was small. The members enjoyed the sermons and classes. They loved to fellowship with one another. They just had become satisfied with just sitting in the pews. Serving others had not been incorporated into their Christian walk. The senior minister acknowledged that "we just were not Jesus to others." Looking at his congregation with compassionate eyes, he knew that the ministry staff and leadership had failed their membership by allowing such a state to develop in many of their brothers and sisters.

To address this situation, the elders and ministers started praying about the situation. Together, they also started studying Mark and John 13–17. Their time together was intentional, as they sought to answer two key questions: "What was God wanting us to do?" and "What did Jesus leave us with?" Around this same time, some of them went on a mission trip to the Dominican Republic. While serving a local church there and reaching out to those in need in their community, a revelation came to the minister: "Why can we not do these kinds of things in our home congregation?" It became clear to him that they needed to be "the hands and feet of Jesus" in their community. "Jesus" became their goal.

To facilitate a change in his congregation, preaching and teaching on how to "be" Jesus in the lives of others became paramount. Also, the ministry staff and the leadership team would need to embrace their new approach and lead the way by actively serving others. A Wednesday night class was developed to equip the membership for service. The topics that were discussed not only laid a foundation on how to reach out to others, but also helped the members of the class embrace this vital need and make positive changes in their attitudes toward these crucial biblical principles. The class covered a sundry list of topics, including the "dos and don'ts" of serving others, what it truly means to love God and love others, what Jesus did and how we emulate Him, how Jesus drew people to Himself, and how to meet people where they are. They even went through my book, *Created for Good Deeds*. After several of these classes, some of the men started going out on Wednesday evening to pray with the homeless in their community. Some of the women made cookies for them to take.

Kickstarted in a new direction, this congregation began to serve. In an outreach effort they called "Good News Bible Club," they used soccer as a medium to get to know those involved at a more personal level. Of course, this opened doors for performing good works in the lives of those involved, as well as sharing the gospel.

They then started to branch out. For the homeless, they had clothing giveaways and occasional food distributions. They would sit in small groups with them to get to know them, share stories, pray with them, and present the gospel. It did not take long before three families were converted. Unfortunately, the city put up roadblocks to their initiative, so to continue reaching out to the homeless, they sought established ministry partners. With Interfaith Emergency Services, they started to serve the homeless breakfast once a month, and like before, they spent time with them to get to know them personally.

The church also started providing volunteers to work with Wear Gloves, an organization designed to impart dignity and worth to the homeless and others in need. Through training, skills development and advocacy, they help the downtrodden build self-esteem and facilitate their ability to earn what they need. Participants learn to generate products, such as producing their own coffee and making fasteners for closet shelves. While the volunteers become the hands and feet of Jesus in this endeavor, they take the time to share Him along the way.

They branched out by becoming involved with two nonprofits that serve at-risk women. For a spouse abuse shelter, they have provided various supplies, such as toiletries, blankets, and towels; they also painted some of the rooms at their facility. They invited the women to attend a weekly Wednesday night dinner and some of the women volunteers shared the gospel along the way. A couple of the attendees were converted, one of whom was a former Muslim. They also have started providing volunteers to His House for Her. Their mission is "to share the love of Jesus by providing trauma-informed practices in a supportive housing environment to meet the physical, emotional, and spiritual needs of at-risk women in recovery."

In still another effort, several of the congregation's elders went to a church in Murfreesboro, Tennessee, to receive training in how to make disciples by using the Discovery Group model. These elders now teach this strategy to others to help develop disciples who fully follow Jesus. They currently have mobilized two efforts that follow this approach. One effort occurs at their own church on Sunday nights. They reach out to disadvantaged inner city youth, picking up some of them and providing them with dinner, a time of worship, Bible study options, and games. This outreach effort includes a caring environment that facilitates a much-needed change in these youth and an avenue to hear the gospel. They also have partnered with the Fellowship of Christian Athletes (FCA) to bring the Bible, Jesus, and God back into their community's high school. The strategy is to use the Discovery Group model to teach discipleship in an FCA club. As long as one of the high school teens leads the group, the activity is condoned. So, some of the athletes are being taught the Discovery Group model to use in these clubs. FCA was so impressed with this church's youth minister having organized this initiative that they made him their regional director.

Regarding his involvement with some of these efforts, the senior minister told me that it was "so satisfying to be Jesus out amongst the people." In fact, only a few times in my life have I heard Jesus' name mentioned more in such a short period of time than in my interview with this gentleman. Yes, Jesus is this minister's goal. Jesus is his Savior. He dedicated his life to share Jesus' Good News and be His hands and feet to serve others. For him, being Christian is being Jesus.

Three weeks after this interview, my friend and minister featured above passed away. What a wonderful legacy he left his congregation! He is one of my heroes of the faith. Jeff, I grieve your passing. I am a better Christian today because of your holy example, godly advice, and servant's heart. Hopefully, this story suitably memorializes a subset of your life's work that you dedicated to Jesus.

QUESTIONS

1. What kind of settings do you find revitalizing? Why is that the case? How often do you take advantage of them?

2. In Psalm 23, what do you think David is communicating in the first few verses about his relationship with God and any results from it? Are you satisfied with your relationship with God in this regard and how might you improve it?

3. Explain the correlations you see between the first few verses of Psalm 23 and Mark 6:30–34.

4. Explain why you take comfort that God and Jesus recognize that we, at times, need rest.

5. How does Jesus view the crowd when He goes ashore at the supposedly secluded place? What does He do?

6. When you are not happy with the behaviors of others, which is more constructive: viewing them through eyes of irritation or care? Explain the results of both tactics.

7. Is there any special instruction that you would like to see offered at your church? How might you go about proposing for such a class to be taught?

CHAPTER SIX

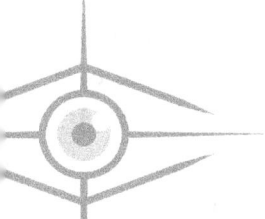

SOME PERSPECTIVES ON WIDOWS

The Lord watches over strangers;
He supports the fatherless and the widow,
but He thwarts the way of the wicked
—Psalm 146:9.

When I was in my late 20s, our congregation formed a slow-break basketball team to play in a local church league. To help make it affordable, the sponsoring church decided to use unpaid referees and required each team to provide them for games other than their own. Such an approach worked out well in the Christian environment of our league. Unfortunately, we only had a few guys on our team, including me, who had an adequate familiarity with the rules to officiate a game, so I was stuck refereeing more games than I would have liked. To be honest, I hated doing it. I had no training in refereeing basketball and tended to watch the game from a fan's perspective. My eyes tended to follow the ball and not pay too much attention to some of the contact that was occurring. My officiating, at its best, was bad.

One Saturday morning, the director of the league called me and pleaded with me to come and referee a fast-break game. One of the scheduled refs could not make it, and he was desperate to find someone to fill in. Normally, our team only had to provide referees for games in our own league, so I was a little apprehensive about officiating a fast-break game. Nevertheless, the need was great, and my Christian ethic moved me to help. In hindsight, agreeing was a huge mistake! Not only was the overall pace much faster, but the competitive level of play was also greater. This compounded my poor officiating skills. My normal bad officiating progressed to awful. Not only did my poorly trained eyes miss a lot of fouls, but the pace-of-play caused me to miss and overlook some infractions that I might have normally called. My best friend at the time was playing on one of those teams, and he got so frustrated with my lack of calling fouls that he looked directly at me and yelled, "Come on Mike, call something, even if it is wrong!!!" If I look back over my life, not too many Saturday mornings are less cherished than this one.

Because of our life experiences, training, biases, environmental factors, and other considerations, our eyes may miss things that others easily see. We may overlook certain aspects of a situation because unfamiliar circumstances overwhelm us. Sometimes, the lack of knowledge and poor communication may leave us unaware of where to focus our attention. Thus, certain things are neglected. I believe such factors were at work in a particular unfortunate incident in the young and developing church in Jerusalem.

OVERLOOKED WIDOWS

Prior to mentioning a specific complaint that arose in the fledgling Jerusalem church (Acts 6), Luke prefaced it with an important observation — the number of disciples in the church was on the rise. I believe this provides us with an important factor into why the issue occurred in the first place. Let's look at the awkward situation that faced the apostles and some important insights that we can take from this incident.

> Now at this time, as the disciples were increasing *in number*, a complaint developed *on the part of* the Hellenistic *Jews* against the *native* Hebrews, because their widows were being overlooked in the daily serving *of food* (Acts 6:1).

The specific issue arose from the daily ministry of serving food to the needy widows of the church. The Hellenistic Jews claimed that their widows were being overlooked by the native Hebraic Jews who were conducting this ministry. Likely, the Hellenistic Jews were Greek-speaking, while the Hebraic Jews spoke Aramaic. Even though, they were all Christian, they probably had separate meetings because of their linguistic differences. Also, the Hellenists made up only around 10–20 percent of the Jerusalem population, so they would have represented a minority group in the church.[35]

Prejudices may have been at work, but probably to a lesser degree. The church was experiencing tremendous growth. From a small group of 120 individuals (Acts 1:15) to 3,000 (Acts 2:41), then to about 5,000 men (could likely double this number to account for women and children) (Acts 4:4). Luke also noted that "large numbers of men and women, were being added to *their number*" (Acts 5:14). And then at the beginning of our verse of interest, he again pointed out that "the disciples were increasing in number." Such rapid growth, though desirous, came with its challenges. Since Hebraic Christians appeared to be overseeing this ministry, they were probably unfamiliar with the Hellenistic widows. Along with their numbers constantly in flux, they had an administrative nightmare on their hands. Because of the two distinct groups, prejudice could have arisen. Nevertheless, the Jerusalem church was known for its sharing, and it appeared that the administration of this ministry needed an overhaul due to the rapid growth it faced.

Whatever the case, we should observe a couple of key aspects about this incident. The problem was real and needed solving. Many of the church's widows required some sort of support to survive, and the Jerusalem church felt it was incumbent on them to meet those needs. In fact, the *importance* of serving these destitute widows was highlighted by the quality of men the apostles desired to spearhead this activity. The church was instructed to select seven men, who not only had a "good reputation," but were "full of the Spirit and of wisdom" as well (Acts 6:3).

In our congregations today, most widows do not face the same kind of utter poverty as some did in the early church. However, other dynamics may be at work that can make today's widow vulnerable. We must be on guard that they are not overlooked. After the death of a spouse, they may tend to withdraw from their normal activities. Remember, many of their life's pursuits were as a couple, and the remaining spouse may now feel awkward attending certain events or even go uninvited. They might still be processing their grief and be self-conscious of their current state and wary of get-togethers. We need to be vigilant, love them, include them, and not let them fall by the wayside.

Jesus' encounters with widows in Scripture were brief, though we can still see how He held them in high regard. These stories make it evident that He empathized with their plight. In the "Illuminating Thoughts" section, we will look into some insights from a counselor concerning the contemporary struggles of widows and how we may be able to help.

JESUS' OBSERVATIONS CONCERNING THREE WIDOWS

Jesus took notice of three widows during His ministry that can help us understand His concern for their difficulties. In each vignette, He viewed them in a favorable light. Unfortunately, no dialogue took place between Jesus and the widows. He only uttered a short, direct statement to two of them. Nevertheless, these statements, along with His corresponding actions, provide us with some important insights into Jesus' perspective of widowhood and the dire circumstances that are often thrust upon them.

The Widow of Nain

Luke left us with one of the more touching stories from Jesus' ministry. Approaching the city of Nain, Jesus, His disciples, and a multitude of the curious made their way to the city gate. Surely, wonderment and joy permeated most of their spirits. Yes, they were tired, and though some among them were skeptics, many of this persistent group believed Jesus was the Christ, a remarkable miracle-worker, a master-teacher, and/or a great prophet. As Jesus and His entourage neared the gate, they encountered a funeral procession heading outside the city. Abruptly, joy met sorrow. Wonderment faced cold reality. The bringer of life faced death. While scrutinizing this dreadful scene, His eyes landed on the tear-filled eyes of a heartbroken woman, and He was moved to perform one of His most gracious and amazing miracles. Let's look at the entire story and draw a few conclusions.

> Soon afterward *Jesus* went to a city called Nain; and His disciples were going along with Him, accompanied by a large crowd. Now as He approached the gate of the city, a dead man was being carried out, the only son of his mother, and she was a widow; and a sizable crowd from the city was with her. When the Lord saw her, He felt compassion for her and said to her, "Do not go on weeping." And He came up and touched the coffin; and the bearers came to a halt. And He said, "Young man, I say to you, arise!" And the dead man sat up and began to speak. And *Jesus* gave him *back* to his mother. Fear gripped them all, and they *began* glorifying God, saying, "A great prophet has appeared among us!" and,

"God has visited His people!" And this report about Him spread throughout Judea and in all the surrounding region (Luke 7:11–17).

Jesus realized that the bereaved woman was a widow, and her only son rested upon the bier (burial plank) wrapped in linens. The text specifically said that when Jesus "saw her" that "He felt compassion for her" (v.13). By gazing into those tear-drenched eyes and seeing the undeniable anguish on her face, Jesus understood the depth of her pain. He responded, not from pity, but a deeply felt compassion. The NASB translation may be a little more accurate than the translators' desired aim. The Greek word for *compassion* is a physical word. It is "felt" in the inner parts of the body (such as the bowels, heart, and other organs). Jesus' heart literally ached for this distraught widow. So yes, He "felt" compassion.[36]

Several years back, my father was terminally ill with prostate cancer. Prior to his diagnosis, he was physically fit for his age, but this debilitating disease slowly turned him into skin and bones over a short nine-month period. I remember walking down the hallway of his home and seeing him shakily exit the bathroom, as he made his way back to his bed. After a couple steps past the bathroom door, he suddenly went down. I immediately ran to his side to make sure he was okay and then compassionately scooped him off the floor. My heart deeply hurt for him in that moment of time. Once a proud, independent man, full of vigor . . . now he barely clung to life, as he humbly depended on others for survival. As I laid him in his bed for the final time, an unrelenting agony engulfed my heart. Even to this day, I cannot escape the tears that want to flow, as I recall that heartrending scene.

I have often heard, "No parent should ever have to bury one of their children." Such a cruel reversal in life brings with it severe and merciless suffering. Luke grievously pointed out that the dead young man in this case was not just one of her sons; he was her only son. Most certainly, her anguish was extreme. God's prophets were masters at the use of imagery, and three of them chose to use the mourning of the loss of an only son as a fitting illustration for someone who endures excessive grief (Jeremiah. 6:26; Amos 8:10; Zechariah 12:10).[37] Jesus became focused on this heartbroken widow, as she painfully made her way to the burial site. We should all take solace in that our Lord is attentive to the brokenhearted.

With her husband already gone, Jesus knew this woman's grief was compounded, because she likely faced an uncertain future. Her whole means of support probably rested with her son. Such widows faced abject poverty in the ancient world due to such circumstances. So, Jesus' compassion may have come not only from a concern for her present loss, but her future hopes could have been dashed as well. Most certainly, her loss was doubly devastating.

As the funeral procession drew near to Jesus, I imagine that He left His group of travelers and made a beeline to the bereaved widow. I am sure Jesus did not yell out His message to her from a distance but sympathetically looked into her eyes and tenderly requested, "Do not go on weeping" (v. 13). Jesus knew the remarkable feat that He was going to undertake, but those listening must have thought, *What an odd thing to say! Let her cry to help her deal with her grief! How inappropriate! He needs to learn how to properly comfort the bereaved.* Little did they know who He truly was and what He would do next. Only a chapter earlier in Luke, Jesus stated to His disciples, "Blessed *are* you who weep now, for you will laugh" (Luke 6:21). He now stood ready to show that He had the power to make this beatitude a reality.

Undoubtedly, silence overtook the crowd as Jesus approached the bier and touched it. Both parties breathlessly looked on as Jesus commanded the young man to rise. As he sat upright, I am sure gasps of astonishment filled the air. When Jesus then lovingly gave the young man back to his mother, the astonishment must have given way to a joyous celebration. Alone no more, this happy mother likely erupted into an uncontrollable joy-filled mix of tears and laughter.[38]

I do not believe that any of us will be raising anyone from the dead, but we can do things to help. Compassion should not bring about dormancy, but the will to act in benevolent ways. If this is not the case, we should ask ourselves whether we are experiencing pity or compassion. Compassion expresses itself in action.

A 'Mitey' Honored Widow

When my graduate degree work at the Harding School of Theology was nearing its end, one of the professors I most respected surprised me with a muted honor. He came up to me at the end of one of my last classes and said, "I would like to ask a favor of you." "Would you mind if I use your research paper for my future classes, as an example of a well-written academic paper?" My jaw must have dropped to the floor. My first paper at this august school resembled what a horrible one looked like. I remember even asking myself at the end of the first semester, *What in the world am I doing here?* I always hated writing papers, and every class I took required at least one of them. I was that guy in class who would raise his hand and ask, "What is the minimum number of pages and citations required?" I did not care much for libraries either, nevertheless, reading the amount of material that would be required. God's transformative work had been ongoing within me for the past seven years I had been at this fine institution, and many changes had occurred in me, both intellectually and spiritually. I now loved frequenting libraries and researching my topics of interest. I also fell in love with the helpfulness and knowledge of librarians and had come to highly regard this behind-the-scenes profession. Most shockingly though, I developed a passion for performing research and writing papers, and now, one of my favorite teachers was asking if he could use one of them as an example. I couldn't say "sure" quickly enough! This did not get announced publicly like my NASA awards, but to this day, it still holds a lofty place of honor in my heart. God's work on me was quite extensive . . . as clay, I was not always pliable. Knowing my less than mediocre beginnings, I am so amazed that God desired for me to write for Him.

Jesus honored a widow in a similar way. It occurred without her even knowing it. Her example would teach an important lesson, not only to His disciples, but to all Christians throughout the ages. Wow, that's truly an honor!

> And in His teaching He was saying: "Beware of the scribes who like to walk around in long robes, and *like* personal greetings in the marketplaces, and seats of honor in the synagogues, and places of honor at banquets, who devour widows' houses, and for appearance's sake offer long prayers. These will receive all the more condemnation."
>
> And *Jesus* sat down opposite the treasury, and began watching how the people were putting money into the treasury; and many rich people were putting in large amounts. And a poor widow came and put in two lepta coins, which amount to a quadrans. Calling His disciples to Him, He said to them, "Truly I say to you, this poor widow put in more than all the contributors to the treasury; for they all put in out of their surplus, but she, out of her poverty, put in all she owned, all she had to live on" (Mark 12:38–44).

As you may have noticed, I shared Jesus' teaching prior to His witnessing the generosity of the widow. He strongly condemned the actions of some of the scribes "who devour widows' houses" (v. 40). In other words, they took advantage of these widows by siphoning off their money for personal gain or mismanaging it. Whatever the case, the result was the same: They drove them into poverty. It seems like no mere coincidence that the next event recorded described an impoverished widow. One thing we know is that this widow was basically destitute. The adjective *poor* was used twice to describe her. Her offering was "out of her poverty," all that "she owned," and her entire livelihood (v. 44). The two coins she deposited were the smallest coins in circulation.[39] The story leaves no doubt that this woman was financially in desperate need. Her clothing likely set her apart as an impoverished widow as well.[40]

Jesus took a seat opposite the treasury located in the Temple's court of women, where 13 horn-shaped chests were located for almsgivers to place their offerings, to watch "how the people were putting money into the treasury" (v. 41). Loud, clanking sounds of the offerings from the rich announced their sizable gifts. In contrast, a barely audible tinkling of the poor widow's two small coins proclaimed her meager contribution.[41] However, to Jesus, the faint ringing of her gift trumpeted something extraordinary. A wonderful teaching opportunity came Jesus' way, and He decided to take full advantage of it.

Life often comes with unexpected incidents that offer us teachable moments. Teaching particular lessons at such times allows them to form deep roots, so we can easily remember them in the future. For instance, around 25 years ago, I decided to move a short stack of black garden pots out of a poorly lit corner of our garage. As I started to reach my bare hand down into the top pot to grasp it, I noticed a small orange object in the dark void of the container. I immediately stopped and took a closer look. Staring back at me through the darkness was a small orange hourglass. A black widow had taken up residence in the pot, and I was inches away from an emergency room visit. As I remember, I called out to my wife and showed her the inconspicuous guest in the pot. I wanted her to see the stealthy spider to drive an important lesson home for her as well.

Similarly, Jesus immediately called His disciples over to Him to take advantage of an important lesson that had just unfolded before

His eyes. He pointed out that the poor widow standing before them was an extraordinary role model for giving. She sacrificially gave, whereas the rich would not even feel a financial pinch from their substantial offerings. Their gifts were from excess; the widow's gift was from deficiency. In essence, Jesus taught that proportion, not amount, determined the value of an offering to God, along with the spirit of giving from which it came. Love for God was evident in the widow's offering. She gave "all" that she had to Him, which was more than "all" the rich people's contributions. For many of the rich, their offering was likely a pompous show. The widow was rich in faith, as she trusted in God to take care of her. Such a lesson was not only given to the disciples for their future teaching opportunities but for their personal benefit as well. Their own finances would likely be strained in the future. So, even if their offerings were small, sacrificial gifts from devout and willing hearts would always be pleasing to God. That's a lesson on which we all need to reflect . . . in whatever circumstances we may live.

Regrettably, this story comes with no dialogue between Jesus and the widow, or any potential outreach. Perhaps, they spoke, but we will never know this side of heaven. Because of this, we might develop an impression that Jesus just coldly used this event to teach an important lesson about giving and had little concern for the widow's plight. I believe this is totally contrary to Scripture. Jesus is the "exact representation" of God's nature (Hebrews 1:3). Their existence is intertwined (John 17:21). God abides in Jesus and works through Him (John 14:10). Jesus submits His will to His Father's will (John 4:34; Luke 22:42). God has great concern for widows (e.g. Psalms 68:5, 146:9; and Zechariah 7:10), therefore, so would Jesus. He voiced His concern in His condemnation of the scribes "who devour widows' houses," whom the widow in our story probably represented. I believe Jesus' concern for the widow is inherent in His description of her utter poverty, but assuredly,

His voice expressed His care, when He said that was "all she had to live on" (v. 44). With the kind of compassion that defines His character, surely such words could not coldly pass His lips but be laced with concern for this widow's situation.

The Widow at the Cross

Rare are the moments in life when we see unmitigated brutality mixed with extravagant beauty. Hanging on a cross in the throes of death, Jesus looked down and "saw" His mother. Surely, He noticed the lines of grief that disfigured her tear-drenched face. Simeon's prophetic words that Mary would also have to endure the torment brought on by Jesus' opposition were horrifyingly coming to pass, as she witnessed her Son's unjust crucifixion — "and a sword will pierce your own soul" (Luke 2:35). One last selfless act of compassion followed from our Savior.

> So when Jesus saw His mother, and the disciple whom He loved standing nearby, He said to His mother, "Woman, behold, your son!" Then He said to the disciple, "Behold, your mother!" And from that hour the disciple took her into his own *household* (John 19:26–27).

Lovingly, Jesus turned over His mother's welfare to His "beloved" friend and disciple, the Apostle John. Embracing His mother with these Words, Jesus wanted her to be loved, cared for, and to experience security as a widow.[42] Like me, you might ask the question, "Why did Jesus not turn the responsibility for His mother's care over to one of His brothers?" His brother, James, was a leader and pillar of faith in the early church. Luke noted that Jesus' brothers were with Mary in the upper room with the other disciples after Jesus' ascension. The Epistle of Jude was likely written by another one of Jesus' brothers. So why entrust Mary to John? Early in Jesus' ministry, His brothers did not believe in Him (John 7:5). Faith in Him as the Christ

Some Perspectives on Widows

and Son of God probably did not come about until after the resurrection, when Jesus appeared to His brother, James (1 Corinthians 15:7). So, at the time of the crucifixion, the brothers were likely at odds with Mary as to Jesus' identity and might not have been sympathetic with her. Consequently, Jesus desired to place His mother's safekeeping in the hands of John who believed in Him and had the character and resources to fulfill such a responsibility.[43]

Even the torment of the cross did not keep Jesus from carrying out His duties as the eldest son by showing compassion toward His mother and seeing to her welfare. What a lovingly selfless act! That is our Savior! That is who He is! He compassionately died on that cross for our welfare. Unquestionably, His care runs deep for each of us.

ILLUMINATING THOUGHTS

James underscored in his letter that "faith without works is dead" (James 2:26). In other words, good works is an essential expression of Christian faith. A properly developed faith should naturally move us to bring God's goodness into the lives of others by reaching out to them, especially in times of need. Listening to sermons and attending classes are important for the development of our faith, but practical applications must follow suit. James considered such a faith that does not result in this as "dead." If such is the case with your faith, you may want to ask yourself a few introspective questions, such as, *Where is my emphasis, to what am I listening, what has shaped my faith, and in what do I truly place my faith?* You may need to make some corrections in some of these areas.

James stressed an indispensable work that highlights the practical part of one's religion.

> Pure and undefiled religion in the sight of *our* God and Father is this: to visit orphans and widows in their distress, *and* to keep oneself unstained by the world (James 1:27).

James did not intend to exclusively suggest that we only help widows and orphans, but they stood in the forefront during the first century of those who were vulnerable and helpless. Today, depending on where we might be in the world, helplessness might also take on other forms, such as homelessness or some single parents.

The Greek word, *episképtomai*, translated *visit* above, involves more than just a social call. A beneficial purpose should accompany such a visit and could include the examination of a situation, provision of help, if warranted, and looking after someone. James assuredly had such an intent here, and that is how the NIV rendered their translation — "to look after orphans and widows."[44]

James identified orphans and widows as those who should show up on our radar screens, specifically those in "distress." The distress that widows may be enduring can come from different areas. For example, they may be experiencing severe financial difficulties, dealing with health- and age-related issues, plagued by unrelenting grief, and lacking the know-how or resources to deal with the situations that they face. We need to help relieve such stressors. We may be able to help with some of these issues, but some of these burdens may be beyond our ability to assist them and may require our congregation's support or other individuals with the skill to help in some matters. Remember, when bringing in outside help, make sure you have the permission of the widow who is experiencing the issues.

A Little Help from a Friend

Dr. Mike Shumate, Ph.D. Christian counselor, has counseled many widows through the years. For the sake of our awareness and practical outreach toward them, I asked Mike to identify three of the more important issues that widows encounter. First, he noted that the *role changes* a widow may face can be quite upsetting and depressing. For instance, many wives enjoy cooking for their husbands. They like to plan and prepare meals that please their loved one. Upon his passing, they lose this much-valued role. This can be further compounded when the last son or daughter leaves the home. The vast majority of empty nesters can tell you of the grief they experienced during the onset of this phase of life, which is compounded by widowhood.

Basically, such shifts in roles are life-losses and will often result in grieving when they occur. By its very nature, a marriage involves a couple. Much of married life is lived out as a pair. A loving partnership should define the relationship of a husband and wife. They dance together. They go out to eat together. They go to church and other church events together. They play games together. They do things with other couples as a couple. They go on vacation together. My wife and I do puzzles *together* when we go on vacation. These activities can be profoundly missed with the passing of our mate, as *couple* no longer applies to a widow's identity. *Widow* and *single* become their new titles and roles in life.

Mike reflected on one of his own recent experiences, as his wife had a short-term stay in a hospital. He mentioned that she always made the coffee in the morning, and he had cherished starting his day by talking with her while sipping away on his morning brew. He said, "We always work on things as a team." Whether it was his research for sermons, preparations for a small group get together, or various benevolent endeavors, they tackled those activities as a team. He felt a deep void while she was away from him in the hospital. With all his training and the counseling that he has done to address this issue, one might expect that some hardening in this area may have occurred in his own life. However, the stark reality of his wife's hospital stay revealed otherwise. In his eyes, I could see that such a thought was disturbing to him and would be a daunting situation for him to personally face.

In first-century Jewish culture, the wife was typically known by the husband. Even today, such may be the case. A lot of wives are reserved and lead quiet lives. Their world may totally revolve around their relationship with their husband, meaning any other associations outside the marriage may be cursory or almost non-existent. We need to take special care to not let such a widow slip through the cracks.

Mike believes that making sure widows have ample associations will be critical for them to successfully navigate widowhood. Members of their congregation can take them shopping or share a meal with them. Encourage them to take classes, join hobby groups, and seek out volunteer opportunities where they can give to those in need. To get them started, we should invite them to participate in such activities or consider joining them in a new pursuit in which we may not currently take part. If your church has a ladies' class, urge them to participate in it, especially since the "couples" concern is nonexistent in this activity. Whatever the case, do not ignore them.

Mike also warned to "not say dumb stuff." Empty platitudes don't help, such as saying, "Everything will be all right," because for them, it may never be all right. Above all else, please refrain from trying to find them a husband. From one of my sisters, I know that such meddling is unwelcomed. Just love them, care about them, talk to them, and in some regards, adopt them.

Mike also pointed out the *financial difficulties* that may suddenly be thrust on a widow. The money coming in may be considerably reduced. Depending on her phase of life when her husband passed, she may be coping with considerable expenses. Monetary obligations for their children's college education, home mortgages, and car payments are some of the more serious burdens she may face. With strained finances, the future may look grave on several other fronts as well. She may ask, "Where am I going to get the money to fix my plumbing problem?" "How can I handle my skyrocketing rent payments?" "With all the inflation we are experiencing, can I even afford my own grocery bills?" Her health may be failing, and she may wonder if she can afford to hire someone to help around the house and the lawn. These problems require money to solve, that she may not have. Obviously, the financial strain may become overwhelming.

We may first think that her family needs to step up and help. Unfortunately, there may not be any family to help. If there is, they may be unwilling or may not have the resources to assist their mother (or whatever the relation may be). In such cases, the church should consider stepping in to help (see 1 Timothy 3:1–16 as to Paul's guidance to Timothy for such situations). This could come in various forms, such as monetary, helping find social and benevolent programs to assist in various capacities, or mobilizing its membership to step up and help in various ways. For church leaders, *compassion* must undergird their interactions with the widow, knowing that they may need to build a trusting relationship with her. Ultimately, she needs a caring *friend* to help her decide how to address the many financial burdens that she is facing or may come up.

Lastly, Mike stressed that widows may *struggle with grief* for some time after the loss of their husbands. Grief varies by the individual, and many models define the possible stages through which one may go. These may involve shock, denial, and anger, among other things. I mention this for the sake of awareness, not analysis, which should be left to the counselors. In due course though, we want to help them get to acceptance. It isn't that the loss will ever go away, but that they have accepted it and learned to live constructively with their grieving.

We may need to be proactive and assist them in obtaining the help they need to work through their grief. A certified Christian counselor can help them constructively address their emotions and what they are experiencing, as well as suggest some productive solutions. They are trained in such matters and are preferred over discussing similar issues with an untrained local minister. A counselor once told me that they needed to undo the poor advice given by untrained ministers on several occasions. Some churches conduct widow workshops and host grief groups to assist them in understanding what they are experiencing, sharing their difficulties, and offering productive approaches to managing their experiences.

Remember to always give widows some time and space to work through their grief. Again, be their friend. Listen! Cry with them! Love them! Be patient with them! When the timing is right, help keep them involved in classes and groups at their church where they can obtain support. Involve them in activities that help others. They will likely find this to be cathartic. Some churches may also find it advantageous to offer a program that teaches some of its membership on how to help others grieve.

Love and compassion are not indifferent.

QUESTIONS

1. Why, and how, might widows be overlooked today?

2. What are some concerns that widows face (in biblical times and today)? How might you help address some of these concerns?

3. Do you think that Jesus was concerned about the plight of widowhood? Explain.

4. How does James define "a dead faith"? How might you address it if you have a problem in this area?

5. How might widows be vulnerable today? What might you do to help safeguard them?

6. Do you know any widows? What needs do they have? How might you help?

CHAPTER SEVEN

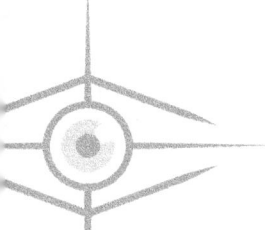

A LOOK OF CONCERN

. . . there is the daily pressure on me of concern for all the churches. Who is weak without my being weak? Who is led into sin without my intense concern?
—2 Corinthians 11:28–29.

At the end of the summer in 2005, our son was heading off to the University of Florida; our daughter was starting her third year at the University of South Florida; and I was finishing up my degree work at the Harding School of Theology. With three of our four family members in college at once, our finances were quite strained. To help save money, we gave our son our small pickup truck to use in Gainesville. After I drove it for many years, our daughter took over at the helm for a few more years. We finally bought her a small car, so my hope was that this reliable little truck would satisfy our son's needs over the next several years. Sadly, during the middle of the first semester, it had a major transmission problem. He gingerly drove it home one weekend, and we went car shopping.

We had hardly stepped foot onto the used car lot, and my son immediately fell in love with a particular vehicle. Its low-profile tires and sporty look had my son salivating. I tried to steer him to another more practical car, but I had already lost that battle. Regrettably, his dream car was a standard transmission, and he did not know how to drive a stick. I knew I could teach him how, but I only had 24 hours to accomplish that task. Against my better judgment, I caved into his love for that sporty little car and bought it for him.

I found the car fairly easy to shift, but to teach that to my son was another thing. He really struggled with smoothly transitioning through the gears, especially the lower ones. After hours of hearing gears grinding and being jerked back and forth as he shifted, we ran out of training time. His rudimentary skills would have to do, because it was getting late. I hardly slept that night, knowing that he would be driving that car on Florida's highways for three hours in the morning. Even though I believed he could handle the car, "stressed out" was the only way to describe my emotions. Early the next morning, he gave us a hug in the driveway, got into the car, started it up, looked up at us, waved by, and started down the driveway with the car roughly surging forward as he shifted it into first gear. As he looked at us for the final time, he surely saw the grave concern in my eyes. I asked him years later whether he remembered the look on my face as he left. He said, "No, but I could picture you cringing in that stressful moment." He did safely make it to Gainesville that weekend and quickly learned to skillfully shift that car.

Looks of concern are a familiar gaze for most of us. Whether on the receiving or giving end of one of those caring looks, most of us have experience with them. When a loved one takes on a new venture or goes down a risky path, those looks of concern typically get flashed and are probably preceded by some sort of advice. We can't help ourselves. We care about them. We want them to succeed. We want them to stay safe. We want them to learn from our experiences and avoid looming pitfalls. Jesus Himself was no stranger to such looks. In fact, He gave one of the most dramatic looks of concern throughout human history. His gaze penetrated to the person's very soul.

DISTANCE WALKING AND AN UNFORESEEN LOOK

Peter followed at a distance (Luke 22:54). Jesus had just been arrested and taken to the high priest's home. Alone, Peter bore the miserable tension between courage and cowardice.[45] He wasn't so afraid that he stayed concealed like most of the other disciples, yet he also wasn't so brave as to demonstrate his allegiance to Jesus as one of the other disciples had done — often believed to have been the Apostle John (John 18:15). In anonymity, Peter stayed at a distance and faced a harrowing trial.

Peter's Trial and Denials

A powerful motivator, fear can forcefully assert its influence on our actions and behaviors. When our view of the future becomes disrupted in troubling ways, or a moment of peril confronts us, fear can produce disturbing fantasies on how things might turn out for the worst. Fear tends to control, not be controlled, once it starts its dreadful work. Let's follow Luke's record of Peter's denials and how fear played a role.

> Now they arrested Him and led *Him away*, and brought *Him* to the house of the high priest; but Peter was following at a distance. After they kindled a fire in the middle of the courtyard and sat down together, Peter was sitting among them. And a slave woman, seeing him as he sat in the firelight, and staring at him, said, "This man was with Him as well." But he denied *it*, saying, "I do not know Him, woman!" And a little later, another person saw him and said, "You are *one* of them too!" But Peter said, "Man, I am not!" And after about an hour had passed, some other man *began* to insist, saying, "Certainly this man also was with Him,

for he, too, is a Galilean." But Peter said, "Man, I do not know what you are talking about!" And immediately, while he was still speaking, a rooster crowed (Luke 22:54–60).

The cold of a spring night in Jerusalem led Peter to saunter over to a fire to warm himself. The darkness provided good cover, but he probably felt the dimness of the firelight would continue to obscure his identity. Nevertheless, a servant girl intently stared at him in the faint, flickering light from the fire, studying his features, and suddenly blurted out, "This man was with Him as well" (v. 56).[46] Peter knew that Jesus may be facing His death in this mockery of a trial (Luke 9:22), and his association with Him could result in grave consequences for himself. Previously, vowing to face prison or death for Jesus (v. 33), he now faced the stark reality of making such a valiant pledge. Earlier, when they came to arrest Jesus, he boldly drew his sword and cut off the right ear of one of the high priest's servants (John 18:10). But Jesus told him to sheath his sword, as what was occurring must come to pass (Matthew 26:54). People often become mighty brazen with a weapon in their hand, but when it is removed as an option, they can turn into a cowering mess. Fear overwhelmed this well-intentioned apostle, and a lying denial sprang from his lips in an awkward attempt to hide his identity.

Let's not be so quick to jump on Peter with both feet. When it comes to declaring our allegiance to Jesus, most of us have followed at a distance at some point in our lives. For example, in attempting to gain acceptance from others, we may conceal our Christianity and practice behaviors contrary to our beliefs. We might not use the appropriate language for a Christian around certain people, nevertheless, mention the name of Jesus. We could feel shame in some of our beliefs, because those around us think they are outdated, misguided, and/or wrong. We live in two worlds, perhaps wearing a mask around our Christian friends. Following at a distance is dangerous business. True faith in Jesus requires our loyalty and should be seen in our actions, behaviors, and language. Walking alongside our Savior may require us to give up certain acquaintances and to stay clear of particular situations. But, by treating others graciously and performing good deeds in their lives, our faith will speak for itself, and we will be rewarded with friendships that we will treasure.

Not much time passed, and another accusation was launched at Peter, "You are *one* of them too!" (v. 58). Troubled by this second allegation, the worried apostle emphatically rebuffed such an idea. He not only denied knowing Jesus, but he also now separated himself from his fellow disciples and their mission. No new challenges came his way over the next hour. Peter might have thought that his deceitful tactics had succeeded in keeping him safe. Yet something about this mysterious man was not sitting right with one of those in the crowd, as he noticed something peculiar about Peter's dialect (Matthew 26:73): "Certainly this man also was with Him, for he, too, is a Galilean" (v. 59). Since Jesus was from the region of Galilee as well, this was an unfortunate and dire development for Peter. His accent gave him away. Peter's curt response was little more than a flailing attempt to deflect the suggestion that his Galilean roots associated him with Jesus. Before Peter could finish his third denial, a cock crowed. Something about that rooster's brash melody surely struck an alarming note in this worried apostle.

The Look

One of the most dramatic scenes in all of Scripture occurred next. Jesus turned and looked directly into Peter's eyes.

> And *then* the Lord turned and looked at Peter. And Peter remembered the word of the Lord, how He had told him, "Before a

rooster crows today, you will deny Me three times." And he went out and wept bitterly (vv. 61-62).

Jesus' look penetrated to the depths of Peter's soul. It forcefully caused the beleaguered apostle to remember the words of Jesus— words he utterly believed would never come to pass. His own words of brazen loyalty surely re-entered his mind as well. His failure engulfed him. He stewed in wretchedness. Alone and lost during this time, the man he desired to be never surfaced. Fear derailed that man, and what came to pass was what he despised.[47]

> "Simon, Simon, behold, Satan has demanded to sift you *men* like wheat; but I have prayed for you, that your faith will not fail; and you, when you have turned back, strengthen your brothers." But he said to Him, "Lord, I am ready to go with You both to prison and to death!" But He said, "I tell you, Peter, the rooster will not crow today until you have denied three times that you know Me" (Luke 22:31-34).

This passage provides for us the context of Jesus' "look." His piercing gaze toward Peter did not communicate anger or hurt because of the denial. Nor was it a stinging scowl that conveyed, "I told you so; you should have heeded my warning!" *Concern* radiated from those compassion-driven eyes. The high priest's minions around the fire viewed Peter as a potential religious miscreant. This lone apostle had just been "sifted" by a master sifter. His faith was shaken to the core. Such contemptible disloyalty and cowardice could lead to this traumatized apostle's ruin. Our loving Savior wanted him to rebound from this shameful event. Yes, Peter sinned, but he did not lose his faith. He still believed in Jesus, His mission, and dearly loved Him. Jesus needed Peter to "turn back" from his fear-laden sin of disloyalty and strengthen his fellow disciples. Satan "sifted" them as well, and they, too, were horribly shaken and hurting (note the "you" in v. 31

is plural; the NASB added "men" for clarity). Jesus' look of concern provided the linchpin for Peter's restoration. Bitter tears needed to flow to lead him down the path of repentance.

G. Campbell Morgan in his commentary on Luke makes an intriguing observation concerning this story: Jesus' heartrending look would have been of no consequence if Peter had not looked at Him. Peter was in the process of uttering his third denial, when the rooster crowed. That shrill call probably continued to echo in his ears for quite some time. You would think that shame would have caused his eyes to veer from the target of His disloyalty. Yet in this moment of dread-filled lying, Peter looked into the eyes of His Lord. Concern met grave shame and sorrow. Beneath Peter's sinful denial, he still loved Jesus, which guided his eyes to His Savior's gaze. Jesus' prophetic words then rushed to the forefront of Peter's mind and vividly came into focus; words that cut him to the quick because of his failure. In times of trial, Peter provides all of us with an important principle . . . never take your eyes off Jesus! The world will try to steer your eyes from Him. Remember Jesus' words, as well! His words can guide us through temptation and lead us to restoration when we fall. Always, always, keep your eyes on Jesus![48]

HE'S GOT THE LOOK

He did not always have "the look." From a young age, my dear friend once saw alcoholics and addicts through the eyes of disdain and fear. Their behaviors intruded into his world in chaotic and destructive ways. Desires that put alcohol and drugs first led them down paths that brought great harm to themselves, as well those they cared about the most. They were ticking time-bombs. Self-control was a lost commodity for them. Nothing good seemed to come from such an existence. Toxic defined their inebriated state. My friend truly feared the destructive chaos that ensued.

His eyes changed. He became what he despised. Eyes that once viewed alcoholics and addicts with disdain and fear became re-oriented. He started to see them as possible friends who would accept him and his craving "to party" and numb his emotional ills. Basically, those who wanted to get drunk and high with him were people he saw as friends. If someone wanted "to party," that guided his sight, which led to caustic relationships. Concerning these "friendships," he said, "They were not truly friends, as we were willing to put one another in danger for the sake of a good time." "It was about the partying, not friendship." A wake of disaster ensued. He had become the bringer of chaos himself.

His eyes shifted again. Drugs and alcohol stopped having the same emotionally numbing effect. "Partying" was no longer fun and only exacerbated deeper problems. His out-of-control behavior created much damage along the way. Nothing seemed to escape the insidious tentacles of his disease. His property, job, relationships, family, finances, spirituality and his own personal welfare all became victims of his abusive behavior. He wanted no more of this hurtful lifestyle and started to look at others through a new lens. Could they help or support him and bring sanity back into his world? Reformed alcoholics and addicts were seen as individuals who could potentially help, but ones still entrenched in that lifestyle were viewed with trepidation. He feared they would bring temptation into his life. He was an addict and always would be. Help came in various forms: Alcoholics and Narcotics Anonymous (AA and NA), a live-in rehabilitation program, concerned friends, and counseling. He drifted along with an inward focus for many years. Much healing needed to take place, and it took great energy on his part to stay the course.

He developed "the look." The day came when he started looking at other addicts with concern. His focus turned outward. He still required some maintenance and attended regular AA meetings and went to church to accomplish that. He was in a good place and realized that he could help others positively navigate their addictions. He started sponsoring alcoholics and tried to help them through the steps of AA. He started volunteering at a live-in rehabilitation facility to help addicts confront their temptation-laden lifestyles and addictive behaviors.

Unfortunately, he had another rough patch of time, when he felt alone and lacked hope. A fellow AA member took him aside in this dark moment. The individual cared deeply for my friend and looked at him through compassionate eyes and spoke a beautiful and meaningful prayer into his life. Its spiritual impact on him was profound. He said, "It was like his concerns were catapulted away; like Jesus saw him drowning and pulled him out of the water like Peter." Memories flooded into his mind of meaningful scenes from when he faithfully followed Christ. He knew there was hope. He needed to adjust some of his thinking. He needed to restore and grow his faith. He came to realize that not only could he help those he sponsored through their addiction issues, but he could bring God into their lives and introduce them to Jesus as well. Having Jesus in their lives had bigger ramifications but would also help them with their addiction issues. That "look of concern" for addicts became Spirit-driven, and his compassion for them came from an even deeper place. He passionately cares for them. I've seen and heard his concern. Whether talking with one of them on the phone or asking my advice on some of their complicated life issues, the concern was real and evident. He shared with me how rewarding it was to help a particular addict mend some of the issues that he had created with his children, ex-wife, and a sister from whom he stole. This caring sponsor helped bring joy and responsibility back into this man's life. Another addict that my friend sponsors has easily learned to detect his look of concern. When the addict innocently (or not so innocently) suggests that he may make a questionable choice, he sees his caring sponsor's eyes transition into that look of concern. Nothing is said; the look says it all. The confused addict detects something is amiss with his choice, so he inquisitively responds, "What?!?"

God is using my friend in a mighty way. He is in the trenches, helping people whom many of us might struggle to view with compassion. I shared this story so that you could recognize that developing the eyes of Jesus, in whatever capacity, may take time. We may encounter some life-changing experiences that help correct our faulty vision, or it may spiritually occur over time. Whatever the case, keep maturing your faith, adjusting your spiritual vision, and becoming more and more outward focused. Compassionately, refocus your eyes to *see* the needs of others and develop the zeal to step in and help.

ILLUMINATING THOUGHTS

Hopefully, your journey through this book allowed for you to peer through Jesus' eyes a little. Each set of discussions and stories were designed to help you understand how Jesus sees things and note where your vision may fall short. To truly be transformed into the image of Jesus, you need to incorporate His perspectives, so you can subsequently act and behave in Christlike manners. Some tweaking to your spiritual eyes may be required, but among God's Spirit, prayer, His Word, and our brothers and sisters, our vision can be corrected and sharpened. Viewing life through the eyes of Jesus will permit us to see people and situations from God's perspective, thus allowing us to properly deduce what actions to take and to serve those in need in righteous ways.

To close out this book, I would like to stay with the theme of this chapter and ask you to reflect with me for a few minutes.

- In your walk with Jesus, are you following at a distance?
- Have you really made a commitment to walk with Him?
- Where do your loyalties truly lie?

- Have you allowed sin to separate and distance you from His loving embrace?
- Do you have vices that you have never addressed or need to be re-addressed?
- Do you have attitudes and biases that distort your spiritual eyes in unhealthy ways?
- Are your virtues aligned with those of Jesus?
- If you gazed up and Jesus turned and met your eyes with a penetrating look of concern, what would be His concern for you?
- What would his prayer be for you?

I'll guarantee that He is deeply concerned for each of us. He could not have gone to the cross and thus be indifferent to the ones for whom He suffered and died. His sacrifice was for all of us.

Those questions were not designed to make you feel guilty, but to help you better understand yourself. Christianity is a developmental journey. We need to be aware of our shortfalls so that we can address them. Walking at a distance is a miserable place to find ourselves. I often offer up this prayer from the Psalms to invite God into the deep recesses of my heart to make evident my shortcomings. Perhaps you will find this useful as well. Let Him in!

> Search me, God, and know my heart;
> Put me to the test and know my anxious thoughts;
> And see if there is *any* hurtful way in me,
> And lead me in the everlasting way (Psalms 139:23–24).

QUESTIONS

1. Can you remember a specific look of concern that was directed your way from a family member or friend? How did you react to it?

2. Why did Peter deny Christ three times? What was his original intention? Did anything occur that might have changed his intention?

3. When Jesus turned and looked at Peter, what do you believe it communicated?

4. If Jesus had *not* turned and looked at Peter, what might have resulted in Peter's life?

5. Why was it important for Peter to weep bitterly over his denials? Did Peter lose his faith? Explain.

6. What are some ways that we might demonstrate disloyalty to Jesus today?

7. Are you able to give others a look of concern that comes from the trait of compassion? Developing compassion may take time, what are some ways that you can help bring it about or increase the degree of it?

ENDNOTES

CHAPTER 1

[1] Gordon D. Fee, *The First Epistle to the Corinthians,* The New International Commentary on the New Testament, (Grand Rapids, MI: Eerdmans, 1987), 647–48.

[2] Mark Labberton, *The Dangerous Act of Loving Your Neighbor: Seeing Others Through the Eyes of Jesus* (Downers Grove, IL: IVP Books, 2010), 75.

[3] Joel F. Williams, *Other Followers of Jesus: Minor Characters as Major Figures in Mark's Gospel*, Journal for the Study of the New Testament Supplement Series, 102 (Sheffield: JSOT Press, 1994), 114.

[4] Hisako Kinukawa, *Women and Jesus in Mark: A Japanese Feminist Perspective* (Maryknoll, NY: Orbis Books, 1994), 42.

[5] David E. Garland, *Mark*, The NIV Application Commentary, (Grand Rapids, MI: Zondervan, 1996), 221.

[6] Kinukawa, *Women and Jesus in Mark*, 46.

[7] Leon Morris, *The Epistle to the Romans* (Grand Rapids, MI: Eerdmans, 1988), 502.

CHAPTER 2

[8] Markus Barth, *Ephesians: Introduction, Translation, and Commentary on Chapters 1–3*, The Anchor Bible, vol. 34, (New York: Doubleday, 1974),150.

[9] Merrill F. Unger, "Heart" in *The New Unger's Bible Dictionary*, ed. R. K. Harrison (Chicago: Moody Press, 1988), 544; and "Heart," in *Dictionary of Biblical Imagery*, ed. Leland Ryken, James C, Wilhoit, and Tremper Longman III (Downers Grove, IL: IVP Academic, 1998), 368–69.

[10] Mark E. Moore, *Encounters with Christ: A Call to Commitment* (Joplin, MO: College Press, 2001), 152.

[11] George W. Cornell, *They Knew Jesus* (New York: William Morrow and Company, 1957), 150.

[12] I. Howard Marshall, *The Gospel of Luke: A Commentary on the Greek Text*, The New International Greek Testament Commentary, (Grand Rapids, MI: Eerdmans, 1978), 697.

[13] Lasana T. Harris and Susan T. Fiske, "Dehumanizing the Lowest of the Low: Neuroimaging Responses to Extreme Outgroups," *Psychological Science* 17 (2006): 847–52.

CHAPTER 3

[14] D. A. Carson, *The Gospel According to John*, The Pillar New Testament Commentary, (Grand Rapids, MI: Eerdmans, 1991), 362.

[15] Gary Holloway, *A Miracle Named Jesus* (Joplin, MO: College Press, 1997), 24.

[16] For a positive view of the neighbors see Carson, *The Gospel According to John*, 365–66.

[17] "Beggar, Begging" in *Dictionary of Biblical Imagery*, 86.

[18] Montonini, Matthew D., "The Neighbors of the Man Born Blind: A Question of Identity," in *Character Studies in the Fourth Gospel: Narrative Approaches to Seventy Figures in John*, ed. Stephen A. Hunt, D. Francois Tolmie, and Ruben Zimmermann (Tubingen, Germany: Mohr Siebeck, 2013), 444–45.

[19] Carson, *The Gospel According to John*, 369.

[20] Beauford H. Bryant and Mark S. Krause, *John*, The College Press NIV Commentary, (Joplin, MO: College Press, 1998), 220–21.

[21] Carson, *The Gospel According to John*, 372.

CHAPTER 4

[22] S. Edward Tesh and Walter D. Zorn, *Psalms*, vol. 1, The College Press NIV Commentary, (Joplin, MO: College Press, 1999), 464.

[23] James Luther Mays, *Psalms*, Interpretation Commentary, (Louisville, KY: John Knox Press, 1994), 231.

[24] Peter H. Davids, *The First Epistle of Peter*, The New International Commentary on the New Testament, (Grand Rapids: Eerdmans, 1990), 125.

[25] Ibid.

[26] F. F. Bruce, *The Epistle to the Hebrews*, The New International Commentary on the New Testament, (Grand Rapids: Eerdmans, 1964), 269–70.

[27] William L. Lane, *Hebrews 1–8*, vol. 5, Word Biblical Commentary, (Dallas: Word Books, 1991), 114.

[28] Colleen M. Conway, *Men and Women in the Fourth Gospel: Gender and Johannine Characterization*, no. 167, Dissertation Series (Atlanta: Society of Biblical Literature, 1999), 148.

[29] Carson, *The Gospel According to John*, 412.

[30] Timothy Keller, *Encounters with Jesus: Unexpected Answers to Life's Biggest Questions* (New York: Dutton, 2013), 50–51.

[31] Mike O'Neal, *Created for Good Deeds* (Nashville: 21st Century Christian, 2016), 82–83.

CHAPTER 5

[32] A. A. Anderson, *The Book of Psalms: Volume 1, Psalms 1–72*, New Century Bible Commentary, (Grand Rapids: Eerdmans, 1972), 197.

[33] Robert A. Guelich, *Mark 1–8:26*, Word Biblical Commentary, vol. 34A, (Nashville: Thomas Nelson, 1989), 340.

[34] D. A. Carson, *Matthew*, The Expositor's Bible Commentary, vol. 8, (Grand Rapids: Zondervan, 1984), 235.

CHAPTER 6

[35] Darrell L. Bock, *Acts*, Baker Exegetical Commentary on the New Testament, (Grand Rapids: Baker Academic, 2007), 257–58.

[36] F. A. J. MacDonald, "Pity or Compassion," *Expository Times* vol. 92, no. 11 (August 1981): 345.

[37] Peter Ketter, *Christ and Womankind* (London: Burns Oates & Washburn, 1937), 334.

[38] James R. Edwards, *The Gospel According to Luke* (Grand Rapids: Eerdmans, 2015), 215.

[39] Allen Black, *Mark*, The College Press NIV Commentary, (Joplin, MO: College Press, 1995), 220.

[40] Peter Ketter, *Christ and Womankind* (London: Burns, Oates & Washbourne, 1937), 362.

[41] Garland, *Mark*, 480–81.

[42] Robert Kysar, *Preaching John* (Minneapolis: Fortress Press, 2002), 134.

[43] Leon Morris, *Reflections on the Gospel of John: Crucified and Risen, John 17–21*, vol. 4 (Grand Rapids: Baker Book House, 1988), 665.

[44] Walter Bauer, *A Greek-English Lexicon of the New Testament and Other Early Christian Literature*, 3rd ed., rev. William F. Arndt, F. Wilbur Gingrich, and Frederick W. Danker (Chicago: University of Chicago Press, 2000), 378.

CHAPTER 7

[45] Fred B. Craddock, *Luke*, Interpretation, (Louisville: John Knox Press, 1990), 264.

[46] James R. Edwards, *The Gospel According to Luke* (Grand Rapids: Eerdmans, 2015), 654.

[47] Clarence Edward Macartney, *Peter and His Lord: Sermons on the Life of Peter* (New York: Abingdon Press, 1937), 95.

[48] G. Campbell Morgan, *The Gospel According to Luke* (New York: Fleming H. Revell Co., 1931), 254.

www.ingramcontent.com/pod-product-compliance
Lightning Source LLC
Chambersburg PA
CBHW070159100426
42743CB00013B/2967